DJs MEAN
BUSINESS

DJs MEAN
BUSINESS

*One Night Behind the Turntables
Can Spin Your Company's Success*

AMANI ROBERTS

www.woodsidemediagroup.com

Amani@woodsidemediagroup.com

ISBN: 978-1-7343466-0-2 (print)
ISBN: 978-1-7343466-1-9 (ebook)

Ordering Information:
Special discounts are available on quantity purchases by corporations, associations, and others. For details, contact Amani@woodsidemediagroup.com or www.woodsidemediagroup.com.

Contents

Introduction 1

10:01 – 10:15 p.m.
Introduce Yourself 5
    Weddings Make Me Nervous 6
    At the Club, Nothing but Stares and Smiles 8
    How Teaching Has Helped My DJ Career 9
    How Did I Get Here? 14
    Thinking with My Head and Not My Heart 16

10:15 p.m. – 10:30 p.m.
Beta Testing/Building Rapport 19
    The Start-Up Business Is Just Like Starting a Set 19
    DJ Beta Testing 20
    The Chicago Marriott and the Latin Mixtapes 22

10:30 p.m. – 10:45 p.m.
Branding Can Change the Trajectory/
The DJ Name (Marketing and Branding) 27
    Branding (A Story) 30
    Marriott Branding: Lifelong Lessons
    on Strong Branding 33

10:45 p.m. – 11:00 p.m.
Troubleshooting 35
    The Seven Most Common Troubleshooting Issues
    a DJ Faces 36

The Ultimate Troubleshooting Lesson 40

The Infamous System Update... 42

The Seven Most Common Troubleshooting Issues

a Business Faces.. 43

11 p.m. – 11:30 p.m.

In the Groove/Preparation Wins Every Time 47

The Beginning of My Record Collection Habit.............. 48

How Music Production Helps.. 52

A Customer Service Lesson 59

11:30 p.m. – 11:45 p.m.

Taking Risks (in the DJ Booth and in Business) 61

A Risky Move to Miami.. 64

Business Risks 70

11:45 p.m. – Midnight

Just Say No to Requests.. 73

Washington, DC, a Second Time..................................... 74

Reinvention in the Business World.................................. 78

Midnight – 1:00 a.m.

Prime Time: A Story... 83

Dallas... 85

Seven Tips to Market Yourself as a DJ 87

Scratch DJ Academy, Los Angeles 92

1:00 a.m. – 1:15 a.m.

The Homestretch 95

Stability... 96

1:15 a.m. – 1:30 a.m.
Avoiding Distractions and Staying Focused 99

1:30 a.m. – 1:45 a.m.
Time for Slow Jams! 103
    Radio Love Song Dedications 103
    Nostalgia in Business 106
    OMG, He Came Back! 108

1:45 a.m. – 2:00 a.m.
The Night Is Over 111
    Uber Confessionals 111
    Don't Go Too Hard Too Soon (Thanks V-Fresh!) 114
    Basic DJ Definitions 116
    Mapping Out a Song 123

2:00 a.m. – 2:30 a.m.
Self-Care 125
    A Strong Tribe 127
    Life Doesn't Happen to You, It Happens for You
    (A Lesson) 129

3:00 a.m.
Reflections 133
    The Climax of the Scratch DJ Academy
    LA Experience 134

Conclusion 139

Acknowledgements 141

To my Dad
Thanks for introducing me to the world of music.

To my Mom
Thanks for introducing me to the world of books.

*"I don't know if being in business has taught me
more about being a DJ or the other way around."*

—Amani Roberts aka DJ AmRo

Introduction

It's midnight. This gig started at 10:00 p.m. and the crowd is *hot*. I'm getting great energy from the crowd. The ages of this club crowd run the full gamut. They are into everything I'm doing. I just played a hot throwback that went over very well, and I don't want to give even a little pause because everyone is under my control. If I keep playing, they'll keep dancing, drinking, and having fun. The club owners are giddy. It's a good thing, too, because a booking agent, who can get me gigs all over the West Coast, is supposed to stop by.

Tonight's performance has been a culmination of everything I've done in business and as a DJ. It's all about connecting with clients and customers. I don't know if being in business has taught me more about being a DJ or the other way around.

I've learned to troubleshoot without letting on there's a problem. I've learned to navigate customer service and built connections with club owners and club goers. I started working for Marriott International as a bellman when I was 18 years old. I worked for the company approximately 20 years in a variety of positions across the country. My business experience at Marriott has helped my DJ craft immensely, and DJing has helped my understanding of business.

Every night runs like the life cycle of a business. The start-up defines my business, grabbing customers by the throat and letting them know I'm here to stay. I can't get complacent—sometimes that means I drop in a classic salsa song in the middle of my set to reinvent myself during the night. It can't get stale; I've got to stay on top of it to expand my customer base and continue to surprise them.

Unfortunately, I just saw the booking agent out of the corner of my eye, and I can see he's heading out the door. That is not good—not good at all!

But I can't get distracted. This is part of the business cycle where the big contract I've been working on for months didn't come through. I've got two more hours to play, and this has been my best set yet. So I'm really going to push it hard right now.

Music is the universal language and has the power to unite people of all backgrounds. DJs are known as some of the most skilled music selectors in the world. The ability to take a group of people at a specific moment in time on a journey through music is a powerful feeling. Helping someone unlock his or her creativity by learning how to be a DJ is similarly powerful.

My goal in this book is to show you how learning various DJ skills is very similar to running a business. These skills can help you work through fear, which is one of the most common creative blocks to DJing and starting a business. Come along with me as I take you through this night of being a DJ, and experience what it takes to unlock your business skills, DJ talent, and creativity.

"Without music, life would be a mistake."

—Friedrich Nietzsche

10:01 – 10:15 P.M.

Introduce Yourself

"First impressions are the most lasting."
—*English proverb*

The Gig Begins

It's 10:01 and I've just dropped the first song at the club in Hollywood, California. When I play the first song, I need to make sure the sound is working properly because that's likely the only time I'll be able to leave the DJ booth. I verify with whomever is running lights and sound that all the speakers are working. Then I can get back to my booth and make it my home for the night. After almost every song, I have a critical method to ensure my success. I observe the room, which can clue me into what the crowd's thinking and where I should go next.

People frequently ask me if I get nervous or feel butterflies before gigs. I have been a DJ since 2008 and have had the opportunity to play all over the world, including in Los Angeles, Washington, DC, Chicago, Las Vegas, Toronto, and Brazil. Throughout my career, I have opened for major R&B acts and played in front of crowds of more than 10,000. I've played numerous places and events, such as

5

clubs, bars, weddings, corporate events, marathons, and experiential events. Whether I use turntables, CDJs, or a controller, I am proficient on all equipment and software and perform a true vinyl set (all records and no computer) a few times a year.

Whenever I play at a new venue for the first time, I get a little more nervous than usual. A new environment with new customers, club managers, security, and bartenders to work with can be a little nerve-racking.

How will the crowd react to my style of music and mixing?

Will they respond to me and keep the dance floor full?

Is this crowd aggressive with the requests?

Will management micromanage me and demand that I play certain songs at a certain time?

After the first 30 minutes of the set, my nerves calm down and it's all good. If I'm playing at one of my normal venues, I'm comfortable in a matter of seconds once the first song begins.

Weddings Make Me Nervous

Ironically, if I have a private event (specifically a wedding), I get nervous every time. DJs have a responsibility to pronounce every name correctly and to play the proper songs at the correct time. It can be a heavy burden to bear.

The importance of hiring a professional DJ for a private

event is not to be discounted. The skill set of reading a crowd, collaborating with an event planner to ensure the timeline is proceeding as planned, and exhibiting overall professionalism is paramount to the success of any event. A DJ who has the experience and training to handle any issues that arise during an event is worth all the money invested in that event. Can the DJ manage all of the sound issues from the equipment at the same time that a stressed-out bride wants to push up the first dance by 30 minutes? Can the DJ handle it when the corporate event planner provides a list of 10 names with difficult pronunciations to be made in two minutes and then disappears to greet the CEO who has just arrived for the keynote speech? Can the DJ satisfy the stage manager who expects the DJ to perfectly perform and announce 30 cues for an awards gala? It is not the ideal solution for the best friend of the cousin who owns a controller and downloads songs from random websites to DJ a wedding or company holiday party or to be the MC at an annual conference.

Understanding how to read the room and making sure that everyone is having a good time is an acquired skill that takes years of practice. If the crowd is not moving to a certain genre of music or a set of songs, the DJ must have the awareness of other genre options and the lack of ego necessary to take a left turn and go in a different direction. Quickly. This is the difference between a memorable night that has the dance floor packed the entire night or a night where people leave early and only remember how good the steak dinner was.

A proper professional DJ is not cheap. The investment and reduced stress are worth two to three times what you will invest in your musical entertainment. I have witnessed events where the DJ just wasn't skilled enough to manage the event, and it ruined the entire atmosphere. I urge anyone reading this book who is debating how much to spend on a DJ at your event to truly invest the proper amount for a professional DJ. You will not be disappointed, and the musical experience will be worth the investment. As one of the famous sayings in the DJ community goes, "Good DJs aren't cheap, and cheap DJs aren't good!"

At the Club, Nothing but Stares and Smiles

When you first start a specific set, people often just look at you. They might smile, they might give you a head nod, but there isn't much verbal communication. It's almost like they're judging a book by its cover, just waiting to see what music you'll play. I wish I could ask every guest whether their expectations match the end result. That would be interesting.

Usually, the room is not crowded yet—people are still coming into the club. You'll want to play a diverse mix of music, like you're warming up an oven; play songs people might recognize and go from there. As you proceed, keep reading the crowd.

How Teaching Has Helped My DJ Career

I am involved in two different types of teaching—teaching a group of college students and teaching DJ students specifically on an individual or group basis. I have individual DJ and music production students with whom I will work one-to-one teaching the fundamentals of DJing and music production. I have a specific curriculum that starts at the beginning of the process and builds a strong foundation as we work our way to more advanced DJing and music production skills. I also offer group classes where we actively participate in the same curriculum in a group atmosphere.

I am also an adjunct professor at California State University, Fullerton (CSUF), where I teach in the Mihaylo College of Business and Economics. I teach juniors and seniors whose majors are primarily Entertainment and Hospitality Management, a class titled Entertainment Money Management (BUAD 360). The focus of the class is to educate the students on how different hospitality and entertainment venues or services (hotels, casinos, amusement parks, e-gaming) earn revenue. We also analyze how money is earned in the music industry (Spotify, Apple Music, YouTube, etc.) and then cross over into television and film (Netflix, Hulu, and traditional films). As we study each section, we also discuss the specific careers involved within the industries we are researching.

Teaching at a college has helped my DJ career by improving my MC capabilities. The trepidation I have felt speaking in front of people has diminished greatly and I am much more comfortable on the microphone. Also, most of my students are between 21-27 years old, so they keep me hip on the popular songs and dances. In class, I can do quick mini focus groups on certain songs or artists that are popular or beginning to be popular as time goes on. For example, one student told me about a new Latin American artist named Anitta whom I had never heard of. It wasn't two days later when a new song was released and featured this artist on the track with a major artist. I have also been exposed to totally new musical genres and different interpretations of songs and dances. *The Running Man* is the most common example of how it looked in 2017 compared to 1989.

Teaching students and showing them what is possible for a DJ in today's business environment is also very inspiring. At first, the students don't realize that what I do is a legitimate serious career. But after a semester with them, seeing the network of people that I know (through guest speakers in class) and the different examples of events and music production projects I finish during the semester, they have a new appreciation.

As a bonus, I bring my turntables in for the final day of class and drop a requests-only set for a portion of class. I start off by walking the students through the role of each piece of equipment in the DJ process by completing a bit of show and tell as I set up the equipment. Next, I ask the students to name a few of their favorite songs and develop an impromptu crate to pull these songs from. Once we get to 10 songs, I start to mix each song together and explain to them my thought process as I mix. *What song fits with the next song in terms of vibe and bpm (beats per minute)? How will I get from one genre to another? Can I be creative and use the effects to accentuate another part of the song?* These are the questions we discuss as I work my way through the set of music they requested. Once this mix is over, I ask for volunteers who want to learn how to do a quick baby scratch and mix in a song. This activity is a highlight of the semester for the students and me.

Teaching has also helped me to deal with and work through the imposter syndrome that I struggled with as my DJ career grew. Many times in my career, my mindset was not in the best place, and as I would get bigger and bigger gigs, a voice in my head would pop up saying, "Who do I think I am by getting these big gigs that other, more experienced and more skilled DJs did not get?"

As I added in the music production portion of my business, there was even more imposter syndrome appearing as I released remix after remix. In the beginning, the remixes were not as polished as what you might hear on the radio but sticking with the motto "done is better than perfect," I would release them. I found myself being afraid to release the remixes because I was scared of what my DJ and music production peers would think. I thought that they would publicly ridicule me, laugh at me, and scold me for putting out a product that was not mainstream radio ready. What I didn't realize was that they were not even thinking about me or paying attention to what I was doing. I also realized that many peers were not doing the same things I was doing, so the simple act of doing the work and putting it out in the universe was far exceeding their level of activity. I was stuck in my own head.

In early June 2018, I received an email from my colleague who was a professor at CSUF. They had a sudden opening for a music industry and hospitality business class and my work experience was an excellent fit for this class. My colleague inquired if I was interested and I immediately said yes. Within two months, I interviewed for the job, completed the background check, and waited to hear if I got the job. Once the official offer was presented to me, I was thrilled to get started. I had a few weeks to revise the syllabus and develop my weekly class lessons.

It was during this process that the imposter syndrome crept in. "How am I with only 11 years of DJ experience (and 20 years of hospitality experience) qualified enough to teach this class at a university level?" At the time, I didn't realize that I was the best person to teach the class, as my years of experience with Marriott and running my own DJ business made me the perfect candidate. Add on the fact that I was still working full time in the industry and could show the students a relevant example of a professional who is still working on his craft and his business and is able to teach them about the industry and use real-world examples.

In addition to chasing away the imposter syndrome monster, teaching helped me with my public speaking skills and the ability to think on my feet consistently. In class, there will be times when students ask questions I don't know the answers to or the structure or planning of the class will be thrown off, and I will have to adjust on the fly without letting the students know I am thrown off.

I've honed my skill of reading the room by teaching college. In my classes, I teach a class that lasts two hours and 45 minutes, which is very similar to a three-hour DJ set. I have to work very hard to keep the students' attention for as long and as often as possible. I do my best to use a combination of interactive activities, group assignments, random questions, videos, and audio cues to keep the students engaged, off-balance a bit, and curious about what is coming next. There are definite similarities to DJing. In the classroom more than ever, I cannot be predictable and boring or students will yawn and doze off. I have to switch things up quickly and keep their attention as best as possible.

There are a few examples of this similar strategy in the business world. Netflix, for example, releases a new show, movie, or returning series almost every week. Adding new content attracts new viewers and keeps regular viewers coming back on a daily or weekly basis. Quick mixing in DJing is very similar. However, when a major release is happening (such as *House of Cards*, *13 Reasons Why*, or *Black Mirror*), Netflix will leave some space around the release date so that no other show competes with it and the focus is on that one show. A great example of this was the 2018 release of *Bird Box* on Netflix right before the Christmas holiday season. This release dominated social media and got a significant number of viewers over a three-week timeframe while

Netflix didn't have any major releases around the same time as this film premiere.[1]

This is just like a DJ letting a popular well-loved song play until the second or third chorus. This applies to "Mo Money, Mo Problems," a popular old-school hip-hop song by The Notorious B.I.G. and Bad Boy Family. People love to hear the third verse where Biggie has his verses. One time while DJing at a club, I switched before the third verse, and a woman came right up to the booth and said, "You aren't allowed to cut Biggie's verse off. You have to let that one ride." Lesson learned!

Teaching students has helped me tremendously with the basics of DJing. Teaching simple tasks such as counting the bars of the verse, chorus, and bridge or mapping out music has magnified my ability to do this for my own DJ sets.

How Did I Get Here?

Quigley's Nightclub – Washington, DC – Years Earlier

On a Saturday night following Howard University's homecoming, my roommates and I headed to a DC club called Quigley's. Quigley's was in the basement of an old bank. The special guest DJ was going to be the famous DJ Biz Markie. I'd heard Biz Markie before, but this was going to

1 Chitwood, Adam. "Why Netflix's 'Bird Box' Release Strategy Was Kind of Brilliant." *Collider*, January 4, 2019. http://collider.com/bird-box-why-netflix-release-strategy-was-brilliant/.

be my first time seeing him at work in a smaller venue with people dancing close to the DJ booth.

Most DJs that came to perform across DC for the Howard University parties had a similar set of songs they would run through with a few gems tucked in there. My roommates and I were skilled at predicting what would come next. We loved to dance, and I enjoyed seeing the DJs at work. I didn't know what or how they were doing what they did but I was interested in seeing more.

Biz Markie started off his set pretty chill, working his way through some old-school hits (Teena Marie, Frankie Beverly & Maze, the Emotions, Run DMC, Eric B. & Rakim) and some new songs that hadn't taken off yet ("Freak Like Me" by Adina Howard, "Fantasy" by Mariah Carey, "Players Anthem" by Junior M.A.F.I.A). Midway through his set, he put together a set of songs that caused me to immediately decide that I wanted to be a DJ.

Most of the kids at Quigley's that night grew up in the '80s watching several of the classic television shows. In the middle of his set, Biz Markie started dropping TV theme show songs from this era and the crowd was mesmerized. He played theme songs from shows such as *The Facts of Life*, *Diff'rent Strokes*, *Golden Girls*, *Fat Albert*, *What's Happening!!*, *The Jeffersons*, *Family Ties*, *Three's Company*, *Sanford and Son*, and *The Dukes of Hazzard*.

We sang along to each and every song and were transformed into our youthful selves within this hot, sweaty, crowded nightclub. It was an amazing experience. When I looked up at the DJ booth, I saw a smile on his face and sweat flowing down his forehead. It was then I decided I wanted to be a DJ. I wanted to give that experience to other people, allowing them to be completely transformed through music.

Driving home in my white Dodge 600 (known affectionately as "the white boy") I tried to figure out how I could make that happen for myself in the future. Cruising down Georgia Avenue, I had crazy thoughts about what I could do to make this a reality. I had no clue where I was going to start, but I knew it was something I wanted to do.

Thinking with My Head and Not My Heart

> *"I've worked in Washington, DC, Atlanta, Chicago, Dallas, Miami, and Los Angeles and followed the DJ/music industry during my entire journey."*
>
> —*Amani Roberts*

About six months later, I graduated from Howard University and headed to Atlanta, Georgia to continue my career with Marriott International. At that time, I didn't think working as a DJ full time was realistic. I was more focused on climbing the corporate ladder. I wanted to have a wife, 2.5 kids, a dog, and a house with a white picket fence. It took me a few years to realize my thought process was way off. As I moved to many of the biggest cities in the United States, the idea of becoming a DJ still sat in the back of my mind.

I moved to Atlanta just a couple months before the 1996 Summer Olympics were set to begin. It was my job to help manage the cafeteria and restaurant inside of the Atlanta Market Center where all the press conferences were held. It was my first management job out of college in a new city. It was a huge adjustment but an amazing learning experience.

I frequented many of the night spots where the best DJs would spin. The Yin Yang Cafe was one of my favorites. I got to watch the Atlanta-based DJs do their thing. It was there I learned how a smaller venue can have a huge impact on the career development of an artist.

The venues I vibed with the most were the smaller lounges and nightclubs. These venues allowed people to get up close and personal with the DJs. It was fascinating to see how DJs moved the crowd. It was easier in these venues to build a group of supporters since they had a more at-home feel compared to the larger clubs.

In Atlanta, I learned to treat everyone I worked with the same no matter their position. I was the assistant manager in a cafeteria and also helped manage a small bar. I spent a lot of time in the kitchen and dish room and at the cashier stand working with the staff. I would manage the cash, prepare the breakfast and lunch foods, and manage the staff. Many of the staff were three times my age. I earned their trust by working side by side with them in the kitchen or dish room or at the cash register. The dish room was often a fun place to work because we had music playing.

I use these lessons when I go to any club or bar and interact with the staff. There is no one person who is more important than the next person. Security at the club is as important as the club manager, bartenders, sound/AV person, and the attendant in the bathroom responsible for getting fresh towels or mints. These are the people who will let you know who your competition is, if there are issues, and if your main client is unhappy or considering making a change. Having a close and respectful relationship with them can be the reason a client hires you again or gives you the first crack at a high-profile project.

10:15 P.M. – 10:30 P.M.

Beta Testing/
Building Rapport

"A teacher who establishes rapport with the taught, becomes one with them, learns more from them than he teaches them."

—Mahatma Gandhi

Rapport (noun) - [ra ˈpôr, rə ˈpôr] - a close and harmonious relationship in which the people or groups concerned understand each other's feelings or ideas and communicate well.

As I get through the first 15 minutes of the night, I want to pay attention to whether people are enjoying the music. Small cues such as tapping their feet or bopping up and down, singing along, or mouthing the lyrics are all things I pay attention to as I get started. It's necessary to find out what will make our customers or prospective customers "bob their heads" or "mouth the words" to our product.

The Start-Up Business Is Just Like Starting a Set

Starting a DJ set is similar to when a new start-up opens for business or an existing company creates a new product or enters into a new space or industry. In business, this is like the beta test of your new business or product. You need to have a few people try the product and determine if your target audience likes it. In other words, you want to see who's bobbing their heads as they experience your sound. If they're not responding to the product or service, what should you do to fix that?

DJ Beta Testing

Let's say we play a certain string of similar classic rock songs. Maybe we start off with a Journey song and the crowd is really into it. Then we might take that song and add on a couple other songs in the genre. We could go from Journey to Bon Jovi to Queen, and then we have played five popular songs in that genre and taken the crowd on a journey through classic rock. Everyone is feeling nostalgic.

They know the words.

They sing along.

We've created a mini moment.

Depending on where we are, we might end with a final song that can really get the crowd singing along. This culmination of our mini set also provides a bridge to the next road we travel down into another genre. When I take the classic rock route, I often end with "Sweet Caroline" or "Build Me Up Buttercup." From there I might transition to pop music, select a Madonna song from back in the day, and then we are off and running into our new genre.

Many of us DJs like to kind of consider ourselves genre

benders—like we can bend and fit different genres together and tell a story, using each genre as a bridge moving forward. The next bridge might be when I play a popular Reggaeton song from pop music and see if the crowd is feeling the genre and in the mood for some more Latin/Reggaeton music. If they are, I can continue along this path with other new and classic artists. I would string those songs together and see if the crowd gives back good energy. If the energy continues to increase, we can continue down that path, mix in currents and classics, and see where this path takes us. If that's not working, we go down another road and see if we can reach the crowd on a deeper level.

I try to start each set with a mixture of old-school classic songs (Rick James, TLC, A Tribe Called Quest) with some new songs people might not have heard yet. We mix the old with the new and explore. Later in the night, the crowd expects to hear the hits, so now is our time to show our range and have some fun with it.

If the crowd isn't feeling what you're playing, it's time to be flexible and meet them halfway. Never take it personally. Be patient. *Did this song get a good reaction from the crowd? Did this song paired with this other song inspire people to head to the dance floor or did it clear the dance floor?*

I get a text saying a booking agent who represents dozens of clubs on the West Coast has decided to check out tonight's show. It's a little bit of a shock but just like in business, I have a product to sell. I need to get this place jumping.

The Chicago Marriott and the Latin Mixtapes

The second stop on my professional journey was Chicago, Illinois. I moved to Chicago to work in a Courtyard by Marriott in Wood Dale, Illinois, as an operations manager. I was responsible for managing the restaurant, sales department, and front desk at this 149-room hotel. I moved to Chicago and knew only one person in the area but that didn't stop me from getting to know the city.

I worked with a great team in Chicago. We were like family. My explorations into the city allowed me to discover Twilite Tone who was DJing at The House of Blues downtown. Twilite Tone would eventually become Kanye West's DJ and achieve international stardom. He's still DJing and producing to this day. I would go to different venues and observe the Midwest flavor of DJing. While living in Chicago, I fell in love with Stevie Wonder's classic song "All I Do" and began to observe the boy band takeover of the '90s with the Backstreet Boys and 'N Sync making it big.

In Chicago, I was first exposed to Latin music (salsa, bachata, merengue, freestyle). Two close friends from work took me to Latin clubs, and I was completely immersed in this genre of music. My love for Latin music has never waned. I consistently add a Latin flavor to as many of my public DJ sets as possible.

In Chicago I learned how different styles of music can bring different demographics of people together. It can transform into pure joy as people get lost in the music and dance.

This is a critical component of being a DJ and in business. You have to know the business and know the competition, because if you want to break the rules you have to know the rules.

This was an important lesson for me. Prior to my experiences in Chicago, I naively thought that although many different demographics of people may enjoy certain genres of music, they stuck to their "hometown" style of music. I was completely off base with this thought process. I was witness to people from all races that were very knowledgeable about salsa, merengue, bachata, cumbias, and freestyle music. This taught me to not prejudge how people look as I determine what type of music will move them as I DJ. It was a valuable lesson being in a room with people from Mexico, the United States, Colombia, Ecuador, Ghana, Puerto Rico, and Chile and learning what the different genres of music meant to them and how they identified with the songs. This was the first time I truly understood that music is the universal language.

Most of my staff in the hotel was from Central America, so I had "on-the job training" with regards to their favorite music, which was salsa, bachata, and merengue. I remember the first time I was sitting in the break room during lunch with a bunch of housekeepers during a regular business day. The housekeepers started to play some salsa music and they asked me if I knew anything about their favorite genre of music. I told them I did not but I was ready to learn. Out came the CD player, and they went out to their cars to retrieve some CDs and begin my education. Over the next few weeks, each housekeeper would bring in CDs of different artists and different genres of their favorite music and play it for me. It was like I was going to music school while I was at work.

Soon it was time for our hotel holiday party, and it was there on the dance floor that I experienced my first salsa lesson in front of everyone. They started with the three basic steps (front/back, side basic, and back basic) and the proper way to count (1-2-3…5-6-7). I would have to follow the leader (one of the housekeepers) as we went through each step on the dance floor. This was my main lesson for that night. It took me a good hour of consistent practice but I eventually got it down. There was no time to learn turns and other more advanced skills, but once again my desire to learn had been sparked. I was like a sponge during every lunch break from that day on.

Meanwhile, my staff at the front desk was bringing me up to speed about freestyle music, which I actually knew more about but didn't realize it at the time. During our slower times at the front desk, they would play different artists on the tape deck we had in our office and share with me where the artists were from and their most popular songs. My staff would also make me freestyle mixtapes that I would take home and listen to during my days off from work.

The highlight of my lessons would be when my staff took me out to a salsa club that also played freestyle music. Once, we were in West Chicago at this small club in the basement of a large building. There was one bar, and the doorman checked IDs and collected the cover fees. If you were driving down the street, you would miss the place as it was hidden in plain sight. There was a mixture of smoke, sweat, and perfume in the air as I walked past the small stage that also housed the DJ booth. I was there in the middle of the club surrounded by hundreds of people in their own world as the salsa, merengue, bachata, and freestyle music pulsated through the speakers and I did my best to put my many weeks of lessons to practical use. I can still remember the sharp highs of the trumpet players from the band playing as the dance floor stayed packed. Many times, I would get caught up watching all the skilled dancers move together with their partners like they had been practicing for years. It was beautiful. When the night was over, I would leave the club drenched in sweat and excited about what I had just experienced. We returned to the club several times during my stay in Chicago, and the experience was memorable each time. At my farewell party before my move to Dallas, I was able to properly dance with several of the housekeepers and put all of their training to good use.

A valuable lesson that I still carry with me today as I manage my DJ business is I cannot do this alone. I need a team who works with me as we cover multiple events across multiple days. I need a team of people who assist me with my marketing, accounting, and administrative work. Even though it took many years for the teamwork concept within my DJ experience to become a necessity, I was able to draw upon my experience working in Chicago. In the business world today, no one is successful without a strong team.

10:30 P.M. – 10:45 P.M.

Branding Can Change
the Trajectory/The DJ Name
(Marketing and Branding)

....

"You too are a brand. Whether you know it or not.
Whether you like it or not."

—Mark Ecko[2]

"Branding can change the trajectory
of your night or your business."

—Amani Roberts

It's 10:30 p.m. and by this time I have played through about 10-15 songs that show my personality. What does each song say about me? Who am I? I love wearing creative T-shirts that allow me to market myself. It could be a shirt that says "I <3 to DJ" or "Slow Jams" or a picture of Sidney Poitier. It all comes back to my personality and branding. Every shirt that I choose to wear expresses a bit of my personality and allows me to share this visual message as a way to get to know me better. In my experience, if you allow

_____

2 Ecko, Mark. Unlabel: Selling You Without Selling Out. New York: Simon & Schuster, 2015.

people to get to know you better in an authentic way, it will create a more loyal following and tribe of people who support your business and musical efforts. Whether it be an adidas® shirt that shows a city that I have lived in, a shirt with a picture of Whitney Houston, or one that gives an ode to '90s R&B, I believe that unique ways of sharing my personality help to confirm my individuality as a DJ.

For most of my corporate gigs, I wear a bow tie. Numerous times, I have my clients and their guests comment on how much they love the bow ties that I wear. It all comes back to my branding. As in the corporate world, it is all about branding. From the colors a company uses for its product to the logo to the music they use in their advertisements, effective marketing can carry a brand.

DJs wear many hats and are responsible for many duties outside of playing music and moving the crowd. We are graphic designers (making flyers for our public gigs), social media experts (tweeting, snapping, and posting up pictures and videos on Instagram, Facebook, and Twitter), accountants (sending out invoices and tracking down vendors to pay us for our work), and even a lawyer here and there as we must use contracts to protect ourselves and our clients.

Through it all, the most important piece of marketing and branding a DJ will do is at the beginning of your career. The DJ name, for example, will follow you as you continue to build your brand. It's a simple act in branding that can unlock different levels of creativity. I always urge new DJs to think of the long game when they create their DJ name.

Will it still be relevant in five years? Ten years? Is it safe (and clean) enough to be displayed on a large billboard in Hollywood? Can a major corporate brand like Apple, Gucci, or Rolls-Royce share your name in their advertisements? While your DJ name should be generally appealing in that sense, it should also show some of your personality. Storytelling is more important now than ever in the marketing and branding space. Make sure that your DJ name tells a good story.

My DJ name is AmRo. I took the first two letters of my first and last name (Amani Roberts) to create my DJ name. One of my close friends started calling me AmRo at the beginning of my DJ career and it stuck. My first name is pretty unique, and the story of how I came up with the DJ name is quick, easy, and fun to share. This DJ name can stay relevant for decades to come.

I have a friend who is a DJ and a full-time dentist. Her DJ name is DJ Flossy. This is a great example of creativity and personality in a simple name. Another option is to use your full name or just first name as your DJ name. After all, you are your brand. DJ Michelle Pesce is a great example of this.

In this day and age of social media, you can always check to see if your potential DJ name is available on various platforms, such as Twitter, Facebook, Instagram, and Snapchat. In addition, I would encourage you to see if the website is available. When I created my DJ name, it was not available, so I decided to make my socials match my company name

(The Amani Experience). I was able to secure @amaniexperience across all platforms.

After you create your DJ name, design a logo. I encourage you to get creative and use your personality. For example, one of my favorite colors is orange so you will see plenty of that color within my logo. I know of one DJ who has the "I" in his logo shaped like a trumpet. That is a great way to show a bit of your personality. Make sure your logo can be placed anywhere as it will follow your DJ career forever.

Branding (A Story)

As I started to get more corporate gigs, I had to figure out a way to stand out through the music. At the corporate gigs, I can't really wear my jeans and creative t-shirts. I have to dress like the best dressed person in the room to ensure people take me seriously and know I am serious about my job.

Bow ties became a staple for me. I began to collect bow ties I had to tie myself and prepared them at every corporate gig. I'd use that as an accessory to help me stand out and make a name for myself. You don't see many DJs wearing bow ties while playing gigs. As the years have passed, I now have people looking forward to seeing which bow tie combination I will wear at my next gig. Guests who appear on my podcast sometimes even send me bow ties as a thank you gift.

I also frequently wear white adidas® Stan Smith tennis shoes with almost all of my suits. They pay homage to Run DMC and how they would rock their adidas® shoes during their shows and videos. The icing on the cake is the song "My Adidas," which was one of my favorite hip-hop songs from back in the day. I knew this accessory was also becoming part of my branding when people began to comment on them at meetings, gigs, and other events. You could say my branding is similar to the big bold red letters within the Netflix logo or the golden arches from McDonald's.

You'll want to keep in mind how you can evolve the look and keep it relevant. Do I switch from the bow tie to suspenders? Do I supplement the bow ties and add text and personal writing to make them even more personal and potentially even more tied to my brand? It's important to keep the distinguishing accessories while moving forward and keeping pace with how the world evolves. Pay attention to fashion trends and discern which ones fit with your style and branding.

Equivalently, businesses can no longer keep the same logo, colors, look, and feel that they had even three years ago. One of my favorite successful rebranding stories is the one involving Old Spice. Old Spice has been around since 1938 and had long been known to be a deodorant for elderly men. That all changed in 2008 when the younger, upstart brand Axe dominated the market by focusing on how using the deodorant could help you attract attention very easily. In the Axe commercials, men would spray themselves with Axe and women would become immediately attracted to them like a magnet drawn to metal. Old Spice had a new goal of attracting the younger demographic of males between the ages of 12-34 who wanted to smell good but not take themselves too seriously. Through some serious branding discussions, the company decided to rebrand their failing brand "Glacial Falls" as "Swagger," which brought attitude and edge to the brand while still expressing confidence. The company believed that these are characteristics that every male wants to exude. The foundation for the campaign was turning wimpy and nerdy men into strong, manly studs. The icing on the cake for this rebranding was the viral videos from "Old Spice Man" centered around the theme "The Man Your Man Could Smell Like." In a series of three videos that went viral, Isaiah Mustafa plays Old Spice Man and goes through a series of witty, rapid-fire monologues expressing the benefits of Old Spice. The creativity of these commercials won numerous awards and is still referred to as a modern-day rebranding best-case example. Credit goes to the agency of Wieden+Kennedy for creating this idea. [3]

When examining the rebranding process, there are many factors to consider. Designs must change. Colors must evolve. Logos must be reinvented to stay fresh in the consumers' mind but say the same thing within the company. It is a very delicate line to walk but it must be done. Take a look at some of the world's most popular brands and how their logos and colors have evolved over the years. A subtle highlight or added color can be the only shift in branding for a few years but it counts as evolution. Change is good

3 Wieden+Kennedy. "Old Spice: Smell Like a Man, Man." February 2010. https://www.wk.com/work/old-spice-smell-like-a-man-man/.

and change is necessary. How will my logo and branding evolve? Stay tuned!

Marriott Branding: Lifelong Lessons on Strong Branding

While working for Marriott, I learned three key factors about branding. First, consistency is key. In order for a brand to thrive in today's marketplace, the products and services must be consistent. With consistency, you increase consumer trust. People buy from people and brands that they know, like, and trust. The second factor is reputation. Reputation is more important than how your website looks, the style of your logo, and the photos you share online. Customers will share the positives and the negatives about working with your business. It is your responsibility to ensure that the positives far outweigh the negatives. The most effective method to market your business is through word of mouth.

The final factor that I learned from Marriott regarding branding is evolution. It is a delicate dance to stay consistent yet evolve at the same time. At the core, your philosophy and high level of service must stay consistent. Your products must evolve to keep pace with the changing times. Marriott started as a root beer stand in downtown Washington, DC. Look at how that company has evolved over the years. As a business, you must be willing to try new things, establish new revenue streams, and pivot if your main business is no longer working in the current day. As the popular saying goes, "Evolve or die."

10:45 P.M. – 11:00 P.M.

Troubleshooting

....

"The cure for the pain is in the pain."

— Rumi

It's about 10:45 p.m. and things have been going well. All of a sudden, a turntable stops working or a speaker goes out. Now it's time to troubleshoot while the music is playing. The issue could be minor—something like you're playing on turntables and the needle gets dusty and stops working. That happens because you're using real record needles and there's dust around and some turntables aren't as clean as others.

Sometimes, speakers will go out either in the club or in the booth where you need your monitors. You'll need to fix it. You'll have to move around the DJ booth to figure out what is going on, but you can't let the crowd know something's wrong because you are still building energy and you have to keep the music going at all times.

That's the number-one rule: ***The music can never stop.***

To fix this, you first slow down and follow the signal flow. Nine times out of 10, this will bring the issue to light and allow you to get back running at the most optimal level. There are two good methods for aspiring DJs to practice fixing tech problems. The first is to completely disassemble your entire DJ set-up and put yourself on a timer for five minutes to get sound up on both sides (left and right) of the turntable or controller. The repetition of setting up the equipment will develop the habit and make signal flow a habit instead of an exercise. The second method is to continue this exercise with a fellow DJ colleague with the goal of trying to stump each other as you have the timer still in effect. The two DJs will go back and forth unplugging different wires, activating unnecessary features on the mixer or turntables, and trying to confuse the other DJ. This exercise is very valuable (and fun) because it always forces the DJ to think outside the box when it comes to researching and correcting the problems.

The Seven Most Common Troubleshooting Issues a DJ Faces

#1 – Your computer crashes in the middle of your set.

Solution: Always have a backup computer, vinyl records (if you are playing on turntables), CDs (if you play on CDJs), or a few songs or mixes downloaded on your phone where you can connect to the mixer via an auxiliary cable. As soon as the computer goes down, move quickly to get some music on while you fix everything.

#2 – A speaker stops working.

Solution: Change out the wires or XLR cords as well as the power cord. Otherwise, put on a long song or mix and swap out the speaker.

#3 – A turntable or CDJ is not communicating with the mixer properly.

Solution: Check the connections in the back and make sure they are connected properly. White goes to white and red goes to red. Depending on if you are using a turntable (phono) or CDJ (CD/line), make sure the cables are connected correctly. Check the grounding wires as well.

#4 – Dusty needles!!

Solution: Change the settings to Internal Mode (where the song will play automatically through the computer with no interface from the CD or turntable) and clean the needle. With advances in technology, dusty needles may be a thing of the past in the next three to five years.

#5 – Someone disturbs or runs into your equipment.

Solution: With the assistance of security, keep the DJ booth as clear as possible. If this happens, hop on the microphone or quickly switch to the first chorus of the song. As hard as you try, there will always be someone staggering into or around the DJ booth to make a request or to share some (hopefully) happy thoughts with you. Create strict boundaries and protect people from themselves.

#6 – No sound!

Solution: One of the most dreaded feelings in the DJ world is seeing the volume level meters rising and falling with the song that is playing but no sound is coming out of the speakers at all. The despair that fills your heart when this occurs is second to none. I have learned to start with the basics and make sure that the Reverse button is not activated. (The Reverse button is a switch that completely reverses the cross fader and channel volumes, meaning that the highest volume is actually the reverse—no volume.) After this, make sure that all volumes are at twelve o'clock and all speakers are properly plugged in and turned on with volumes up. The majority of the time, these solutions will fix the issues.

#7 – Your monitor stops working.

Solution: Most DJs rely on a monitor (additional speaker where they hear how the mix sounds to the regular crowd in the club or bar) to properly mix as well as control their levels (the volumes of each track they are playing). At various gigs throughout a DJ's career, this monitor will stop working in the middle of a gig, which means that you are DJing "blind." I recommend swapping out the power and XLR cords to the mixer. If this doesn't work, you will have to mix through your headphones and then immediately take your headphones off after each new song to gauge the levels. Make sure you don't see any red (song clipping) on your volume levels.

I recall a time period when I was DJing for a newer club in

Beverly Hills. We experienced a brief power surge, and this temporarily knocked out all sound and lights. When I realized that the club was completely dark for a few seconds, I quickly went into emergency mode. Before the power came back on, I unplugged the USB connection from the mixer to my computer as well as my power cord. The power came back on and the mixer cycled back to being on. As I restarted the computer, I grabbed a vinyl record from my bag and put on a song so we could get some music going. This worked well as the front four speakers started playing the music, which put the crowd at ease and saved the vibe that I was previously building. To my horror, however, the monitor and four additional speakers (including the sub-woofer) were not working anymore. This was a huge issue as the club was without sound in some parts and no bass at all on the dance floor. We need the bass for optimal dancing conditions. I saw the bar manager working furiously at the house sound controls to no avail and the stressed look on his face was deepening as the seconds ticked by. As the record I initially put on was more than halfway over, I was able to restart my computer and connect it back to the mixer via USB.

The song "Rapper's Delight" by the Sugarhill Gang is a good song to keep in the back of your pocket for moments just like this. The song is almost seven minutes long. It is recognizable enough and people enjoy a quick old-school, hip-hop flashback. Therefore, the crowd will usually stick with it for a while. This song will play on and will allow you to take an extended amount of time to try to figure out and fix things. I dropped this song, exited the DJ booth, and headed to the front four speakers. I turned off the speakers and unplugged the power cord from one speaker, turned down the speaker volume (to avoid popping when the speakers come back online), and waited 15 seconds. I did that for each speaker. I plugged the power back in and slowly increased the volume on each speaker until I heard music. It took about five minutes overall, but we had full sound up except for the monitor in the DJ booth. By the time I got back to the DJ booth, I was able to mix right into the next song and then get to work on fixing the monitor. The same strategy I used for the additional speakers worked on the monitor and we were back in business. Although the time elapsed was approximately eight minutes, the audience only experienced about 20 seconds of no music, which was a great recovery! At the end of the night, the bar manager was especially appreciative for my quick thinking and assistance in fixing the problem.

The Ultimate Troubleshooting Lesson

My first experience with just how important troubleshooting is occurred during my time as a DJ student at Scratch Academy Los Angeles. Scratch DJ Academy is like a college for DJing with students of all ages attending to further their DJ knowledge. It was the final exam for the entire program. We had arrived at Scratch Academy at 9:00 a.m. on a Sunday in March. This semester, I had done about average on my previous five sets, which are like mini exams leading up to the final exam. I needed to get a strong score on this exam to pass the class. The exam was set up so each student had to play a 20-minute set at the time period corresponding to the time it would be at a club during the night. For example, if your time was 10:00 a.m., you'd play like it was 10:00 p.m. at the club. If a DJ before you had played a specific song, you could not play this song. The song was "burned" and could not be used.

About 15 other students, also taking the exam, made up the audience. The instructors graded us on everything from our mixing skills (how well you blend from song to song), microphone skills (how well you speak on the microphone during your set), programming (what songs you choose to play at what time), and presentation (how you were dressed, how you connect with the crowd during your set, and your facial expressions and eye contact during the set).

I was set to play at 11:40. The hardest part about this exam was the waiting. I got more stressed and anxious as my time approached. I had to scrap a couple songs other students played before me. My friend from class was playing his set right before mine. It was 11:35 and he was working through his final songs for his set. I set up my computer and Serato Box to swap out. All of sudden, the sound cut out and the music stopped.

We scrambled quickly, trying to follow the sound and discern what the issue was. Minutes went by and still no sound. A few of our brave classmates tried to help to no avail. Our lead instructor stopped the class and offered a reward for anyone else in the class who could get sound up.

No one could. Then our instructor stepped to the stage and simply turned the mixer on and off again and the sound came back. I quickly began my set and tried to make the best of it, but my mind was not in a good place. I am sure my face showed the stress as well, and my mixing skills were not up to par. My DJ mentor was there watching, and it did not go well. It was one of the most embarrassing moments of my DJ career.

This lesson in troubleshooting sticks with me today, many years later. If I had slowed down and taken more time to analyze the issues, I could have solved this problem on my own. I could have used the microphone to talk to the crowd briefly while I turned the mixer on and off again. But I had to go through that experience to learn how to handle problems when they come up. I'm glad I had the chance to learn it in a classroom setting.

The Infamous System Update

One time, I was excited to get access to the new dark mode on the latest update and spent a whole afternoon upgrading my iOS. I was completely naive as I arrived at my gig 30 minutes before starting time and plugged my computer into the mixer. To my absolute horror, it would not connect.

I switched the USB ports and wires, rebooted the computer, and did everything else I could think of. It would not work. I checked the time and it was 9:50 p.m.; the internet searches for a fix didn't have a solution that would take less than two hours. I was in big trouble. Due to the troubleshooting classes I went through at Scratch Academy, I had a backup laptop with me *and* a backup hard drive with a significant amount of music. Luckily, this laptop had not been upgraded to a new OS, and I was able to connect to the mixer and get music going right at the call time of 10:00 p.m.

The next challenge to fix was that I had no current music on my hard drive, as it had been full for eight months. I took the first hour (while I was playing the opening set) to transfer a collection of 30 current songs one by one to the backup laptop via Airdrop. This tedious task had to be accomplished while I was going through the very steps I've described, which was the ultimate challenge. I survived the night with a successful set, but I cannot recall a more stressful night of DJing in my DJ career. The next day, I bought a new hard drive, backed up my DJ computer, and then reinstalled a later OS. Never again will I upgrade to the most current iOS.

The Seven Most Common Troubleshooting Issues a Business Faces

#1 – It offers too many products or services (especially at the start-up of the business.

Solution: Niche down and focus on being excellent with one service or product before expanding.

#2 – It grows too fast without proper support.

Solution: Read about companies that have scaled up successfully and learn the process they followed. There are also scaling coaches who specialize in this space. The right coach can save you millions of dollars.

#3 – A business runs out of money.

Solution: Watch your hiring cadence and be diligent with your finances. Outsource as much as possible, which saves significant cost and allows more flexibility when pivots are needed.

#4 – The main product or service doesn't sell while a secondary product or service does sell; yet the business owner does not see the trend.

Solution: Pivot, pay attention to what people are asking you for, and go for it. YouTube initially started as a video-based dating service ("Tune In, Hook Up") where users could upload short videos describing their ideal partner and browse for potential matches. After seeing the potential in a broader online video hosting service, it made a pivot and is now the premier video hosting site in the world.[4]

#5 – A business spends too much time watching the competition.

Solution: Don't compare your business to the competition. Stay in your lane and adopt the abundance mindset by

---

4 DeMers, Jayson, "5 Big Brands That Had Massively Successful Pivots," Entrepreneur, (February 15, 2018). https://www.entrepreneur.com/article/308975.

recognizing that there is enough out there for all of us. This is difficult but necessary.

#6 – A business hires the wrong people.

Solution: Be diligent about who you are hiring and take the extra time to fully vet the potential new team member. Consider outsourcing specific tasks before hiring someone full time. It is very expensive to hire a new person after previously hiring the wrong person.

#7 – A business underprices its services.

Solution: Know your worth and do your best to stick to it. In the beginning, you will need to be flexible, but as you get more experience, your value increases quickly.

> *"Know your worth. Then add tax."*
> *—Anonymous*

The lesson for this chapter is that when resolving issues, you first have to slow down and deliberately work your way through the troubleshooting checklist; yet at the same time, you have to go very fast because you need to resolve the issue quickly so that you can get back to normal. I think that this has numerous parallels to business because you always need to keep the business running but you have to slow down to properly diagnose the issues. You don't want your customers or clients to know that there are any issues but you still have to fix issues quickly because you need to get back up and running at your optimal level as soon as possible. Many businesses have suffered worse issues because they have rushed to solve every type of issue without taking the time to properly diagnose the main issue.

11 P.M. – 11:30 P.M.

In the Groove/
Preparation Wins Every Time

....

"The blessing of being able to write music and let music speak for itself is you let the melodies and let the lyrics and the groove talk to people instead of me talking to people."

—*Babyface*

By the time I hit 11:00 p.m. in the club, I've hit my groove. As the crowd trickles in, I have to convince them to stay at this club rather than investigate other options for the night. Preparation can save a DJ here.

People will often ask me how I keep track of all the new music released across the world. I remember visiting Waxie Maxie record stores every Tuesday afternoon to see what new records or tapes were released that week. They used to have a bulletin board announcing the dates of new album releases with the artists' names written in felt pen along with the date. From there, I became obsessed with The Wiz, a bigger record store with CDs and countless aisles of music to discover. Today, music discovery is much easier and denser than ever before. I use various sources such as Spotify,

YouTube, and Apple Music playlists as well as Reddit forums, blogs, and meetups with other DJ colleagues. A valuable, yet hidden, resource for my personal music discovery has been other guests or patrons of clubs and parties that I work. Compared to the past, in our current environment, the DJs may not be the first people to discover a song. The power is now with the people. I have learned to talk with people and ask them to send me their playlists on different platforms along with recommendations. This has been a great resource for learning about new artists and other music that could translate over to clubs, lounges, bars, and other public performances. As a lifelong learner, I am an open book when it comes to music research and programming. I welcome feedback and recommendations from music enthusiasts who are in venues where I am playing. There are no better people to learn from than people who are dancing (or not dancing) to what I am playing. Music discovery is a full-time job and is crucial to maintaining your authentic sound as a music selector.

The Beginning of My Record Collection Habit

The first CD I ever purchased with my hard-earned money was Jodeci's "Forever My Lady." I stopped by The Wiz record store in College Park, Maryland and raced home with my purchase. During high school, I worked as a bagger at Snyder's Grocery Store in Silver Spring. The tips I acquired from working this job allowed me to start growing my CD collection at a rapid pace.

I recall a specific release of a CD that I waited on for almost a year. I saw the movie *Boomerang* in theaters during the first week of release and the soundtrack was a fast purchase for me immediately after watching the movie. I loved all of the songs on this soundtrack, but there was a song by then-new artist Toni Braxton that really caught my ear. "Give U My Heart" was this song and it was Toni's first single. I couldn't wait to hear what else she would come out with and so I began to ask about her potential album release date and mark my calendar.

I learned a valuable music industry lesson while waiting for Toni Braxton's album. Many times, albums are delayed due to new songs being added, samples being cleared, or just timing. My patience was rewarded, though, as this album is considered an R&B classic debut album, and I still own the very CD I bought back in 1993.

The depth of my musical collection and knowledge taught me the importance of using this knowledge to prepare for each set. As I prepare for a weekend full of work, I will prepare every day by digging for music to make my sets sound unique, fresh, and familiar, yet new at the same time. In many instances, the digging and collecting doesn't happen as you might expect it. Often, I will be driving in the car and hear a song on XM Radio that serves as a tickler for me to add it to my next set. There are also times when I am watching a TV show or movie and hear a song that sparks a memory and I have to add it to my upcoming set list. *Scandal*, the TV show, was great for that. I also remember hearing the song "The Night We Met" by Lord Huron on the Netflix show *13 Reasons Why*, and I had to save it and play it at a high school prom. (The song went over very, very well as the kids ran to the dance floor and had a massive group slow dance.) My ears are always open, listening for new music that I can creatively use in my various DJ sets.

I like to compare the art of song curation to a mad scientist who is in the lab testing out different formulas to find a cure for the common cold. A scientist will try an infinite amount of experiments to create a cure. To date, we have yet to find a cure but that has not stopped the research from continuing daily. As a DJ, it is hard to get 100 percent of the crowd to dance for the entire time of an event, party, or night out at a club. That is the ultimate goal for a DJ but almost impossible to achieve (like curing the common cold). However, each night we test out how different songs work played together and at what time of night. When new songs are released, normally we bring the audiences along slowly, as it is still rare for a new song to be ready for prime time right off the bat. Oftentimes, we have to mix a new song with great potential in between two popular songs to show that, in our opinion, the new song has the potential to be as popular as the songs before and after it have become. We like to call this the "sandwich method."

Whether it is watching a television show, listening to a radio show, or going to the latest movies, new songs can be found anywhere and everywhere. The app Shazam, favoriting on YouTube, likes on Spotify, and simple screen shots or notes on the phone is how the curation process starts. After discovery, we buy the song from our record pool (a resource for DJs that allow us to download music legally from a service that record labels partner with to share music from different artists), Amazon, Apple Music, or directly from the artist's website. Then we plan when and how we will share this song with the public during our sets. After acquiring the song, we test it out in public many times and observe how the crowd reacts and the best times to play the song.

There are a few questions that we always try to answer as we listen for a new song. Does the song have a chorus that prompts people to sing along? Are the verses easy to understand and create simple moments for people to sing, chant, or rap along? Does the beat continue throughout the entire song and allow people to dance continuously with no breaks? How is the drop (the time period in a song where it reaches its highest point in terms of energy)? Are there words in the song that allow the DJ to have some fun with a bit of word play? Is there a sample from an old-school song that can be used to introduce this song? This is a process that is repeated daily for DJs. There is never a time when a DJ's ears are not open and listening to a song and wondering, "How can I use this during my next set?" There is no perfect formula in terms of song curation that will work every time in every venue, just like there is no 100 percent cure for the common cold. However, consistent song curation can get you very close to having that dance floor 100 percent full almost 100 percent of the time.

These stories about song curating and preparation allow me to be uber-prepared for the 11:00 p.m. to midnight timeframe when I have to string old and new songs together to keep the crowd involved and engaged. Taking a risk and trying out a newer song early in the set will pay dividends during my next set as I will know whether or not it will work. DJs are no longer the gatekeepers to new music, but we can use our experience as music curators to share new music and classics during a set. Preparation is key, but it doesn't happen an hour before the set. It is like a river; it never stops.

How Music Production Helps

Being a music producer in addition to being a DJ helps me add different elements to my daily sets and allows me to play unique remixes of popular songs with different edits and mashups. That can further add to my signature branding moments. I attended Scratch DJ Academy to learn the techniques. Many of my mentors and advisors said it would be useful to have general music production skills to create original music, remixes, and edits of popular music. I finished Scratch DJ Academy's Music Production program in 2015.

For the final exam, we were tasked with creating four original songs and releasing an EP. I wanted one of my close friends to sing a bit on a track that I would present at the graduation. This was crucial to the success of my final project because I wanted an actual singer to be on my track to add a higher level of legitimacy to my first work of art. I was taking my new skills of music production seriously and I wanted people to take notice of this. Also, I had known my friend since she was five years old and had watched her career blossom. I thought it would be amazing to finally work together on a song, as music was one subject that continued to bring us closer. I prepared five different tracks for her to review and determine which one she would want to sing on. I sent her links to the "finished" tracks and requested that she pick a song and then send me back vocals that I could add to the song and include it on my final EP. I was so excited that I was going to have a dope singer and close friend sing on my track. I visualized describing the process during our final presentation in front of over 200 people and watching their faces express amazement as they listened to the track that I made. I was halfway to a Grammy moment in my mind!

When I sent my track options to her, I wasn't prepared for the rejection. She told me the tracks were nowhere near harmonically correct for her to sing on and she couldn't do it. While it was ego crushing, it was also true. It taught me another valuable lesson—I needed to learn more music theory, which would help me ensure that any original music or remix I produce would sound harmonically correct.

I cringe to go back and listen to my first remix that was created back then, but the progress I have made since that moment has been staggering. I now know the proper chords to use in each song. I know how to finish musical sentences within remixes and original songs. I understand the concept that the best part of a piece of music is in the silences. I continue to learn to not overproduce individual songs and that keeping things simple is many times the best solution.

This music theory process has taught me some invaluable skills. First, I practice my piano in the morning for 35-45 minutes six days a week. This discipline habit has transformed the rest of my personal and professional habits and has added in a meditative element to my daily routine. I also formed a remix group with my mentor and piano instructor (V Fresh) called A Starter Jacket. The name gives homage to the jackets that were big in the '90s, as our style of remixes gives a '90s hip-hop and R&B vibe. We released one 10-song remix EP in August 2017, another 11-song remix EP in January 2019, and our third remix album in January 2020 which has 13 songs on it. We have attended the ASCAP Conference in Hollywood since 2018 and continue to learn numerous skills and meet several potential partners. We now produce radio-ready edits and remixes, which is a far cry from my first EP I released for graduation. Even my friend, Teresana, who first told me to learn more about music theory, has commented on my improvement.

Now one of the best feelings is playing my own remix while at a club or a bar. I think back to the first time I played one of our remixes out at a club. For months before, I was scared to even play one of our remixes in public. It was later in the night and time to bring the energy down, as the night was almost over. This was the time when I love to drop in some down-tempo slow jams to bring the night to a close. The song was "Honey" by Kehlani, and we had created a remix from the acoustic version of the song. We added in a creative drum pattern for the beginning of the song and then a Latin rhythm break during the chorus. We also added additional percussion and bass underneath the acoustic guitar that was already present. The final touch was a bit of reverb on the vocals with some delays as we entered the chorus. I decided to go for it and mixed in our remix right after a very popular song and then played another popular song right after it (the sandwich method!). I brought the song in, took my headphones off, and watched the crowd react. My heart was beating fast and I was super nervous! To my extreme delight, the crowd stayed on the dance floor and continued to groove with the song. A good number of people recognized the song and were singing along. I was smiling throughout the entire song and even shot some video of the people enjoying the song to send to my re-mix partner. The icing on the cake was after the night was over (about 15 minutes after our remix was played), three different people came up to the DJ booth and said, "We recognized that song by Kehlani but had never heard that version. Who was it and how can we get a copy of that?" My smile was even larger as I told them that I had made that remix with my partner and if they gave me their email, I could email them a copy.

After getting over my nerves, I learned that I can sneak in one of my remixes between two popular songs and observe the crowd's reaction. Are they grooving to the remix? Do they recognize the lyrics and the original song? The best reaction is if the crowd continues to dance and move around, which means the remix blends in and you have accomplished the goal. A smaller bonus is when you see people out on the dance floor dancing but they have their phones out and are using Shazam on the song to discover the version they are hearing.

Another notable remix success story occurred when we remixed the artist Niia and her song "Nobody." I discovered this song through one of my weekly Spotify playlists and it caught my ear. As I kept listening to the song on repeat, I began to brainstorm different elements I could add to the song so that I could play it out in a club or bar. Heavier drums, a riser, some sweeps, and perhaps a drop would be good additions. I floated the idea to my remix partner and we decided to go for it. The first step we took was to speed up the song from 102 bpm to 108 bpm. Next, we added the heavier drums so it would have some punch if it was played on a larger sound system and would encourage more dancing. Additionally, we added some pickups near the end of the music phrases, which would make the transitions from intro to verse to chorus less predictable and more exciting. The artist's vocals in the song were perfect so the only thing we added was a touch of reverb and a delay here and there. Once we added each element, panned a few of the sounds (adjusting the sides where we hear the sounds to more left or right speaker), and mixed the song, we sat back and listened. Every once in a while, we will create a remix and it just comes out almost perfectly. We call this type of remix "the one." Somehow, the beat we made, the edits to the song structure, and the simple additions we made caused the remix to flow extremely well and sound fantastic. This quickly became a remix that I would play out at lounges very frequently and people responded very favorably to it. Heads would bob up and down, feet would tap, and we would see the blue screen of the Shazam app make an appearance. I was even able to drop it in during a club set and it fit. People stayed on the dance floor, continued to dance, and got lost in the song. Rarely will I have a song that qualifies for the lounge and the club but this was one of them.

Normally, we don't put much stock into what happens in the social media world. Our typical strategy is to share all of our work across the social media platforms, tag the artist where appropriate, and move on to the next remix. It is a fact that artists will get overwhelmed with comments, questions, and tags from millions of fans across the world. This time was different. We added the song and got to work on our next remix. Two days after we shared the remix, I got a notification on Twitter and Instagram that Niia's official account had retweeted our remix as well as liked our post on Instagram. I was over the moon! Immediately, I took a screen shot and sent it to my remix partner. This was a small bit of confirmation that we were on the right track, and it inspired us to keep creating. This social media "win" let us know we belong and filled our creative cups for months to come. We rode this social media high for a good amount of time and have experienced similar wins from other remixes we have completed. The feeling never gets old and continues to leave breadcrumbs of inspiration as we travel down this creative path.

Many businesses start off offering only one service and end up adding to their list of offerings as their business evolves. McDonald's started off selling burgers and fries, and they now have full breakfast (all day!), lunch, and dinner menus. Netflix started as a DVD-lending company that would mail its customers DVDs to watch and return when they were done. Now this company is a leading media conglomerate that is focused on streaming services. (Netflix still offers the option of getting DVDs mailed to you.) Apple used to be known only for its computers. I remember learning programming on an Apple IIc at Takoma Park Middle School. Now Apple is one of the leading sellers of cell phones and tablet devices and the sales of its watches are on the rise. These three companies all showed that in order to survive in the business world, you must evaluate market demands and add product offerings that match with your brand.[5]

Successful music producers have also evolved through the times to stay relevant. Dr. Dre first started producing tracks like "Before You Turn Off the Lights" by the World Class Wreckin' Cru, which was known as electro rap. He evolved and birthed the genre known as G-Funk and the rest is history.

The act of my learning and then using music production to add to my business is a similar example. This skill allows me to stand out from my peers and also gives me additional

5 Greiner, Andrew and Ivory Sherman. "A History of McDonald's Breakfast." *CNN Business*. February 11, 2019. https://www.cnn.com/interactive/2019/02/business/mcdonalds-breakfast-history-timeline/index.html.

business services to offer potential clients. Do you need original music for a commercial you're creating? I can make that for you. Do you want to learn how to use a DAW and create original music? I can teach you. Would you like a remix made of one of your most successful songs to extend the popularity lifetime of that song? I can do that. You must be present in the market, evaluate the best product offerings to add, and then move quickly to address them.

In the business world, preparation is key. The most successful businesses never stop preparing.

> *"Luck is where opportunity meets preparation."*
>
> —*Seneca*

A Customer Service Lesson

I think back to my Marriott days and from the very beginning, preparation allowed us to provide exemplary customer service and create lasting impressions. From my first days at the front desk when we would book guests their favorite rooms, to researching VIP gifts for meeting planners coming to the hotel for a site visit, to designing and completing an owner's deck, we constantly needed to be prepared. I have countless stories of how preparation allowed our sales team to stand out from our competition.

One of my favorite stories involves a client we had come to visit our hotel in Arlington, Virginia. This client was particularly interested in making sure her conference attendees

had easy access to the museums in Washington, DC but
not be too close so that the conference would lose attendees
to the general sessions and breakouts. In addition, this
client wanted to have authentic crab cakes as a prominent
part of the menu throughout the week. To prepare for this
site visit, we had several curators from museums such as the
National Air and Space Museum, the Hirshhorn Museum,
the Holocaust Memorial Museum, and the Treasury
Building join our site visits at different parts of the tour
and share a quick one-minute speech about their museums
and why we were the perfect location for the meeting. At
different stops throughout the tour, we offered crab cakes
cooked in different ways. Broiled mini crab cakes, baked
jumbo crab cakes, crab cake soup, and even a crab cake and
custard dessert (it was amazing) were part of the food tour.
The client was quite impressed and booked her group with
our hotel. Preparation won the day with this client.

11:30 P.M. – 11:45 P.M.

Taking Risks
(in the DJ Booth
and in Business)

....

*"If you're not willing to risk, you cannot grow, and if
you cannot grow, you cannot become your best, and
if you cannot be your best, then you cannot be happy.
And if you cannot be happy, then what else is there?"*

—*Les Brown*

*Should I play this new song that has the potential to break out
into a big hit even though some of the crowd might not know
the song?*

*Should I try this new scratch I have been working on as I make
my transition into the next song I am playing? If I mess up,
could it destroy the vibe I have built in this club tonight?*

*Should I switch up the genres real quick and sneak in some sal-
sa music even though the crowd is feeling the hip-hop journey I
am taking them on?*

Many creative experts will tell you fear is the biggest inhibi-
tor to creativity and has prevented some of the most creative
minds of our time from being as productive as they would

have liked. An act as simple as beginning to write a book, create a new song, or paint a new painting can be stopped in its tracks by fear. As several of my music instructors have told me, "You have to learn the rules before you can break the rules."

The first element of the DJ lesson is learning a simple baby scratch. Many people are afraid to touch the turntable and the record, worried they will permanently scratch the record or produce a terrible sound. This simple lesson can be applied to other aspects of a creative venture. Afraid of starting that painting that has been on your mind for weeks? Take a brush and complete the first few strokes on the paper. Have you been procrastinating writing that novel you've talked about for years? Sit down at your desk and write the first paragraph. These actions are analogous to getting behind the turntable and completing a simple scratch. As famous author Anne Lamott says, "Do it bird by bird..." Touching a turntable and scratching a record, especially in front of peers for the first time, can be nerve-racking.[6]

My first time beat juggling in public was quite stressful. A simple way to describe beat juggling is when you start the song on one deck (the left) and then after one bar (four beats) you start the song over again on the opposite deck (the right). From there, you cut the time in half to two beats on the left and then two beats on the right. You continue to reduce the time and some of the most talented

6 Lamott, Anne. *Bird by Bird: Some Instructions on Writing and Life.* New York: Pantheon Books, 1994.

DJs can go down to eighth or sixteenth notes. I am not there yet but future goals! I had planned to use the classic Ginuwine song, "Pony," baby scratch in and then juggle over one measure, two beats, one beat, and then let the song continue. This had been part of my practice routine for weeks and I decided to try it early one night at a club. I am embarrassed to say that my heart was racing and my hands were also shaking when I got started. I was able to get the one-bar beat juggle down and a portion of the two-beat section down, but then it fell apart and I had to let the song ride. The funny thing is that no one in the crowd knew what I was trying to do and they didn't know that it fell apart. Only I knew. I actually had a feeling of relief that I had tried the trick. I wanted to try it again right away, but I had to wait for my next public gig. The adrenalin rush I caught was addicting! This initial experience didn't deter me from trying again on future occasions. Eventually, I got the mini routine down to one beat and am working to get the eighth notes portion locked in. If I had never taken a small risk, I would not have experienced any growth. Growth is most important in any career and business.

Eventually, when you are mixing back and forth from song to song, you will have to just go. Whether you quick mix (mix in and out of a song after the first chorus) or wait until the final outro of the song, you will eventually have to go. Yes, the song might not mix well. Yes, the beats could be off a bit. Yes, the crowd could still be feeling the previous song. You still have to move on to the next song and continue the journey. The simple act of bringing in a different song is a small risk but it is a risk that must be taken. On average, most DJs will play between 120-160 songs a night within a four-hour set. It is a common, yet unwritten, rule that every hour (60 minutes), a DJ will play each song an average of one minute and 45 seconds. If you do the math, this breaks down to approximately 34 songs per hour. Over a four-hour period, this will equal to approximately 136 songs. If you factor in a bit of quick mixing here and there, this amounts to 120-160 risks that we take each night. Nothing ventured, nothing gained.

> *"Fear is always triggered by creativity, because creativity asks you to enter into realms of uncertain outcome. This is nothing to be ashamed of. It is, however, something to be dealt with."*
>
> —*Elizabeth Gilbert in Big Magic*

A Risky Move to Miami

When I decided to move to Miami, Florida, it was a very risky professional move. I gave up the status of being a general manager of a hotel and became a sales manager at a full-service hotel, the 620-room Biscayne Bay Marriott in downtown Miami. My thought process was if I take one small step back I can take two giant steps forward in the future. This is what actually happened.

I decided to move to Miami because I had fallen in love with sales and there was an open position in that city. I was attracted to the city of Miami because of the weather, the diverse population, and a plethora of fun activities to do on a consistent basis. The lack of state income tax was also a bonus.

Once again, I knew not one person in this city but I decided to move anyway. I remember driving from Dallas to Miami and coincidentally Will Smith's song "Welcome to Miami" was popular at the time. As I drove down Interstate 95, this song was on the radio. How serendipitous! Looking back, moving to Miami was one of the top five most significant and positive risks I have taken in life.

While working in Miami, my sales skills became even more refined, and I learned about how to sell a destination and a city that had somewhat of a negative reputation. How does that help me in my current role? Many times, people have had negative experiences with DJs that they have used in the past. Either they have used DJs who have been noncollaborative (they just want to play the music *they* like), have been unprofessional (drinking while on the job or dressed inappropriately), or have given a poor presentation. I have to first repair their negative perceptions, and then convince them to invest in their program or business and spend the proper amount of money on a DJ for their event. We had to do the same thing when we were selling the city of Miami first, and then our hotel. The city of Miami was just coming off the tragic incidents that involved the murders of tourists who rented cars in Miami and many meeting planners were staying away from the city.

Our sales team was super focused on accentuating the positives of the city and going above and beyond with showing how much the city had to offer in addition to our hotel. We had to be creative with our proposals, and when a site visit occurred, it was time to get outside the box and design an experience for each potential client. The experience I attained from designing experiences for my clients in Miami is the core focus of my business now.

The Amani Experience is about making musical memories, and the team-building activity we do is all about having a nostalgic and team-building experience through the activity. We once brought a large pharmaceutical client to Miami as we were bidding on a program with them. We chose to take a mini cruise from our dock at the back of our hotel and around Star Island, Fisher Island, downtown Miami, by the Port of Miami, and then over to South Beach, and have this client experience by boat what our city had to offer. We ended our tour with a personalized meal prepared by a partnering restaurant on South Beach with individual meals prepared for each guest. The attention to detail and research helped us meet the clients' needs while showing them a whole new (and safe) side to the city, and we were able to book the business.

The skills of research and attention to detail are paramount for me to apply as I continue to distinguish myself from the crowded sea of DJs. Working with clients on a corporate level involves numerous hours of research in terms of their goals for the event and musical desires and "do not plays." The research may involve following them on Spotify or

Apple Music and observing their music-listening habits and the playlists they have created. For extreme research, I may hop on social media and see what songs they are talking about, liking, and promoting. The information I ascertain can be immensely valuable and impressive to clients. I then apply all of the details discovered as I construct a proper playlist to work through the specific night.

Another important customer service skill set I learned in Miami was building a list of specifications for each client. By coordinating with the client's admin assistant and designing unique VIP gifts for their arrival, we were able to stand out and be forward thinking when it came to the client gifts. We would call the admin and ask about our client's favorite magazines, candies, drinks, snacks, TV shows, musical artists, movies, etc. Once we got this information, we would use this data to design an amazing and relevant VIP gift with a Miami twist to it and have it ready for their arrival in their room. The attention to detail really set our hotel apart from our competitors and elevated our level of service.

How does this apply to the #DJLife today? On a simple scale, if I have a client who loves Debbie Gibson, Michael Jackson, and Tone Loc, I will be sure to mix in plenty of those songs throughout their event. If I am at the club and I know that someone in VIP is a big Kehlani fan and also really enjoys old-school hits from Bad Boy (Carl Thomas, Mase, 112, and Biggie), I will be sure to mix those songs in throughout the night.

Paying attention to small details throughout the night as well as being selfless will elevate my level of service even while DJing at a club. One time, there was a birthday at the club and the birthday girl loved Young Jeezy. Instead of just playing one Young Jeezy song ("My President"), I decided to play a fourplay of Jeezy, including a few duets ("Soul Survivor"), which still fit with the night and the rest of the crowd did not even notice. The birthday girl was thrilled beyond belief. This is a small example of attention to detail and making this client's experience memorable.

Think about how you make each interaction with a client a memorable experience. People remember how they feel, and the better you can create fun and memorable experiences with each interaction, the better. Are you having a pitch meeting? What can you include in the pitch meeting that will create an experience that is memorable? Do you use the favorite colors of the client? Intro the pitch with a favorite song of the client? Use a clip from a favorite movie as part of the pitch? Use what you know about the client to make each experience memorable.

Mango's and Jazid were two of my favorite spots in Miami to observe musical acts and DJs who were heavy into mixing Latin American hits with the current hip-hop and pop music hits. Even as I was living in Miami, I was still only an observer and not a participant. In the back of my mind was still that desire and dream to be a DJ but fear of the unknown held me back. I recall many nights inside of Jazid (on West Washington) where so many of the popular musical acts would play and consistently move the crowd. I was there in the early days of Jazid before it got to be really big and artists such as Prince would perform there.

It was at Jazid where I witnessed firsthand how different acts would engage with the crowd and consistently move the crowd through their music and microphone work. When you entered Jazid back in the early 2000s, the musical acts were right at the front of the bar, and they almost served as a front man or woman for the club in terms of attracting the street traffic to enter the restaurant and have a few drinks. Immediately when you entered, the musicians would smile and literally give a welcome as they continued with their songs. As their sets continued, the groups would mingle among the crowd and get to know each patron of the bar and then weave each individual's stories into the journey they were taking us through during the set. This simple act was challenging, as the club was not very large and the crowd was forced to get up close and personal as more and more people entered. What was even more impressive was that most acts were generous with the microphone and encouraged people to sing along if they were covering a hit. One Saturday night, a request went out in the crowd in search of someone who could sing in the key of F-major because the musical act needed some assistance with an original song they were preparing to perform. I have learned that there is always a singer in the crowd and this time proved me correct. Their original song required a three-octave arpeggio to be sung during the chorus, and within two minutes of warmup, the guest volunteer was ready to go. Once the original song hit the chorus, the harmonization combined with the high energy from the crowd as we rooted on this volunteer singer was a sight to behold. I remember getting goose bumps as I was a witness to this impromptu performance. The song was only four minutes but most of us in the crowd wished that it would continue for double the time. The guest singer was overwhelmed with emotions and had tears streaming down her face as the song came to a close. It was amazing how different acts continued to find unique ways to read, get to know, and involve the crowd, and I have never seen a similar environment in my career.

It is ironic that I never once saw a DJ at Jazid, but I learned so much about reading a crowd and feeding off the energy before my DJ career even began. At Mango's, I witnessed, participated in, and learned the power of crowds dancing together with the visual motivation and inspiration of professional dancers. If you have ever been to Mango's on Ocean Drive in South Beach, you know how the dancers there can literally move the crowds. The bonus of spending many evenings there was the education on all of the Latin genres of music (salsa, merengue, bachata, cumbia), which was a crucial building block as I moved closer to the genesis of my DJ career.

Business Risks

In business, it is the companies that take risks and succeed that become legendary. Businesses of all sizes must take risks or eventually they will become irrelevant. I have plenty of stories and examples of companies that take risks and end up propelling themselves to higher levels.

One of my favorite stories of taking a risk is about Sara Blakely and her brand known as Spanx. Sara used her 15 minutes with a buyer from Neiman Marcus to go to the women's bathroom and show this specific buyer how her Spanx product worked and how convenient it could be for women all over the world. This quick but major risk got her the Nordstrom order, and this propelled her business to eventually become a billion-dollar company by 2019. She took a simple, split-second risk that worked out.[7]

Another that comes to mind is popular singer Amanda Palmer. Tired of dealing with the restrictions that come with a major record label, Amanda decided to travel down a different road to fund her upcoming album. She used crowdfunding and a membership site called Patreon, where she was able to offer her fans different monthly perks for joining her campaign. This had never been done before, but Amanda decided to take a risk for a better result for her art and her career. She has since funded several albums and now has a loyal and passionate fan base that supports every one of her projects.[8]

7 Howes, Lewis. "Sara Blakely: Spanx CEO on Writing Your Billion Dollar Story." Episode 397. https://lewishowes.com/podcast/sara-blakely/.

8 Millman, Debbie. "Design Matters from the Archive: Amanda Palmer." *Design Observer.* May 15, 2017. https://designobserver.com/feature/design-matters-from-the-archive-amanda-palmer/39584.

We are back in the club and midnight is approaching. The energy level is increasing and the room is getting packed. I have just worked through a nice five-song mini set that has set me up to enter the prime-time stretch of music at the perfect spot.

I glance around the room when I get a moment to see what the agent who stopped by is doing. I can't find him. Did he really just come for a few minutes and leave? That would not be good. I am working the crowd up to a nice frenzied level and he isn't here to see how I build a set throughout the night. My heart sinks and I feel like my date went to the bathroom and never came back. The show must continue so I dig deeper into the music. I find a piece of joy in each song I play to distract myself.

11:45 P.M. – MIDNIGHT

Just Say No to Requests

....

*"When you say yes to others, make sure
you are not saying no to yourself."*

—*Paulo Coelho*

In my opinion, the second most difficult part of being a DJ is managing requests in a way that leaves the people making the requests happy even if I choose not to play their songs. In many of the venues I play, the DJ is right in the middle of where the crowd is so there is easy access to the DJ with limited security. I have had to learn how to manage requests while still playing music. I would be a wealthy DJ if I had a dime for every time someone said, "If you play this song, I guarantee you the entire club will love it and dance for the entire song" or "It's my friend's birthday and they want to hear this song right now before we leave." If the request fits, I will try to work it in, especially if we have not yet hit prime time. For example, if we are going down a '90s R&B pathway and someone requests some Aaliyah or SWV, that makes sense and I can work that in. If we are going down a West Coast hip-hop pathway and someone requests Mack 10 or Warren G, I can make that happen. It makes sense. However, if we are going down the current top-40 pathway in prime time and someone requests Billy Joel or Shania Twain (it has happened, and I do love Billy and Shania), it just doesn't fit in. The skill of being able to say no while making them feel like I am saying yes is one I'm continuing to develop.

One time, I had just dropped "Hypnotize" by The Notorious B.I.G. and the crowd was feeling it. A young woman came up to me and said, "You should play 'Killing Me Softly' by the Fugees next. It fits…" I smiled at her and told her I would think about it. As the song kept running, I thought about it and she was right! It would fit. So I quickly cued the song up and mixed in on the next chorus. The crowd loved it and sang along to most of the lyrics.

The time before you get your first request is the calm before the storm.

In my life, my second time living in Washington, DC was the calm before my storm.

Washington, DC, a Second Time

I got promoted to director of national accounts at the Crystal Gateway Marriott in Crystal City, Virginia. As I headed back "home" to DC, I was still uncertain about how I could start my DJ career.

I moved back to DC on August 20, 2001. The hotel was less than a mile from the Pentagon. We all know what happened on September 11, 2001. I was living in the hotel at that moment when the plane hit, and it was something that

I will never forget. As a hotel management employee, we were tasked with directing hotel guests from the lobby to the ballroom on the second floor, which was the designated safe place for all guests. At the same time, we were waiting to see where the fourth plane would land. Rumors were that it was headed to the White House. It was a stressful 90 minutes until it was reported that a plane had crashed in Pennsylvania. I will never forget the smell of burning fuel and layers of smoke streaming into our hotel (along with people fleeing) on that tragic morning. People from the Pentagon came into our sales offices to use our landline phones or email accounts to contact their families and friends notifying them that they were safe. There was a constant flow of people walking across the 14th Street Bridge, which was a crazy sight to see. The fire trucks ran back and forth past our hotel for weeks after this happened. The news crawl on CNN debuted after this tragedy, and we were constantly overwhelmed with stories and information. A few of the most valuable business and life learnings from this hotel and time in DC were recovering after a traumatic experience. These lessons have stuck with me throughout my life and DJ career. I learned how to handle adversity without my life coming to a crashing halt.

We had to keep attempting to book business for this hotel when people had no desire to travel and visit any high-profile cities. Inside the nightclub, there will always be a bit of adversity throughout the night, whether it be via troubleshooting (see "Troubleshooting" chapter) or plain old issues. Sometimes, you'll have a large group in the club that decides to leave, which means potential revenue loss for the club. Other times, the headlining DJ does not show up, shows up late, or shows up incapacitated and is unfit to get on the deck.

One time, I worked at an LA club that spent six weeks advertising a guest DJ appearance with radio, print, and social media ads. The line was around the corner for people who had prepaid for entrance into the club. The guest DJ showed up so drunk and high he couldn't stand up straight, let alone get on the decks and begin to blend two songs together. I was warming up the crowd and getting them ready to go crazy when the headlining DJ appeared onstage to take over. Club management decided the DJ was unfit and had to decide how to share this with the crowd.

Management decided to tell people the headlining DJ was sick and that everyone in the club would get free vouchers to attend a future show of their choice. I had to hop on the mic and share the news with the crowd, "I have some good news and some bad news. We will start with the bad news first. I am sorry to say that our featured DJ is violently sick and unable to perform today. We want to ensure you stay healthy and they have been quarantined. The good news is that you will get free admission to a future show of your choice, and you get to rock with *me* the rest of the night. I promise to make it worth your while if you choose to stay. Thank you and let's go!!" Right after the announcement, I dropped a current hit that everyone was in love with and we were off and running. Making this announcement was nerve-racking but it had nothing to do with me. I made the announcement and then I did my best to keep all the patrons happy. As much as we anticipated the worst, the end result was not nearly as bad. The crowd stayed full until last call. That was another valuable lesson in handling adversity. Needless to say, that specific DJ was not invited back to any one of the clubs belonging to the owner of that nightclub.

Handling adversity in the #DJLife is very similar in the business world. Take responsibility for the issue, be honest with your customers, and figure out the best way to get these customers to focus on the future.

Remakes, renovations, and sampling are popular in the DJ world and in the business world. Mark Twain famously said, "There is no such thing as a new idea. It is impossible. We simply take a lot of old ideas and put them into a sort of mental kaleidoscope. We give them a turn and they make new and curious combinations. We keep on turning and making new combinations indefinitely; but they are the same old pieces of colored glass that have been in use through all the ages."[9]

During my time at Marriott, I learned about the value and benefits that a renovation can have on your business. While I was the director of marketing of a suburban Marriott Hotel, we began the renovation process and had the exciting task of reinventing our hotel in front of us. Taking

---

9 Mark Twain. *Mark Twain's Own Autobiography: The Chapters From the North American Review.* University of Wisconsin Press, 1990. https://www.goodreads.com/quotes/843880-there-is-no-such-thing-as-a-new-idea-it.

something old and making it new is an old marketing and branding strategy that often works out well. A simple analogy is taking an old song during a set and playing a remix of the song or playing a newer song that samples the old song. That's reinvention (sampling) in its finest form.

Reinvention in the Business World

Has your business become stale and in need of a refresh? Do you need to add some new business offerings?

A prime example of a reinvention (or figurative renovation) is Apple's comeback in the early 2000s. In 1997, Apple was on the verge of bankruptcy and was forced to make some drastic changes if they wanted to survive. Throughout the next three years, Apple partnered with Microsoft to release an updated version of Microsoft Office for Mac (which included a $150 million investment from Microsoft). Next, Apple launched the legendary iMac, which had a transparent frame where you could see all of the computer parts. Apple was able to tread water and continue to grow momentum until two major releases launched the company into a new stratosphere in 2001. The Apple Stores were launched, and soon after, iPods were released. Then iTunes was introduced to the public, and this new music portal changed the music industry as we know it today. We fast forward to 2007 when the first iPhone was released and the rest is history. In 10 short years, Apple redefined, renovated, and practically relaunched their entire brand while still operating.[10]

In the hotel world, ownership groups do not allow us to spend 10 years renovating a hotel. A hotel cannot survive an extended period of revenue displacement from rooms, restaurants, and meeting spaces being out of order and unavailable for purchase. At the most, hotel management teams will have six to nine months to renovate.

At the hotel where I was employed then, we changed the entire lobby as well as every guest room, completely changing the look and feel of the hotel. We used new colors and furniture in the rooms, new menu and design of the restaurant, and a brand new, more family-style lobby. The timeline of this renovation took approximately eight months, as we experienced inventory (new furniture) delays and weather challenges.

As a DJ, you can reinvent your brand with a new logo, a new set of equipment for mobile DJing gigs, or a new facade for portable gigs. My favorite example of a DJ reinventing himself is Z-Trip. From a very young age, Z-Trip was rocking parties from coast to coast, including getting paid by his high school to rock his own prom (he still has a picture of the check from his school). As he matured in

---

10 Shontell, Alyson. "The Greatest Comeback Story of All Time: How Apple Went from Near Bankruptcy to Billions in 13 Years." *Business Insider*. October 26, 2010. https://www.businessinsider.com/apple-comeback-story-2010-10#2008-the-app-store-is-unveiled-along-with-trackpads-with-multi-touch-technology-12.

his career, his superb taste in music across multiple genres led him to create the mashup movement. Z-Trip didn't stop there. He linked up with famous rapper-actor LL Cool J and began to tour across the world filling stadiums to maximum capacity and serving audiences across a wide variety of demographics. True to form, Z-Trip has continued to evolve as his partnership with LL Cool J includes redefining satellite radio programming with his radio show on the SiriusXM "Rock The Bells" channel. Looking back to when Z-Trip started his career, there are not many of his peers that are still around and in the DJ game. His ability to continue to redefine and reinvent himself has allowed him to stay at the highest level of DJing.[11] [12]

While living back in DC, two things happened to push me closer to making my move on my DJ career. First, I went to a club that was in the basement of a building in the Georgetown section of Washington, DC. From the outside, the club looked like a normal business located inside of an old-school rowhouse in Georgetown. You would enter through the front door, pay your fees, and walk down approximately 30 flights of stairs, and then the room opened up to a large underground club with the DJ booth elevated from the floor in the very middle of the club. Bars were

11 Stevens, Kyle. "Z-Trip Talks About His Legendary Career in an IEDM Exclusive Interview." *IEDM*. October 25, 2017. https://iedm.com/blogs/onblast-edm-blog/dj-z-trip-in-an-iedm-exclusive-interview.

12 Roberts, Amani. "Ep 57: Z-Trip." *The Amani Experience Podcast.* August 19, 2018. https://www.amaniexperience.com/podcast/ztrip.

located at three of the four corners of the club with a VIP section circling the exterior of the dance floor.

At this club, this was the first time I saw a DJ using his computer to DJ and not carrying crates of records. I kept looking for him to switch out the vinyl records during his set but it never happened! I couldn't grasp this fact at first and it blew my mind. This DJ also had a unique style of mixing (based on my experience) where he would play the chorus or beginning of the next song for a bar and then switch back to the song that was playing, giving the audience a clue of what was coming next. This technique he used was very smooth, clever, and increased the energy from the audience from song to song. His style was fascinating to me, and I have never forgotten my reaction as I stood in the audience.

The second event was my father's sudden death in July 2004. This caught me completely off guard and taught me that tomorrow is not guaranteed. I decided that if I wanted to pursue something, I shouldn't put it off until tomorrow. In a little less than four years, I decided to pursue my dream of being a DJ.

MIDNIGHT – 1:00 A.M.

Prime Time: A Story

....

"If music be the food of love, play on."
—Shakespeare

A Christmas Story

The value of playing the right song at the right time in prime time is invaluable. It can set you up for an amazing night of DJing.

One of the best examples of this was this time when I was DJing at my normal residency in Venice Beach. It was the Friday after Thanksgiving and people were in the club celebrating and preparing for the upcoming month. It was a festive crowd vibing to the music, dancing, and giving out some strong energy. I worked my way through some classic songs, some hits, and even mixed in a few holiday songs ("Santa Claus Is Coming to Town," "Last Christmas"). The clock quickly approached midnight and I wanted to make a proper segue into the popular hits of the current day by using a popular holiday song to make that transition. For some reason, I had "All I Want for Christmas" by Mariah Carey on the mind and thought a few of the people in the crowd would enjoy it and sing along. I prepared to drop that song next, and I thought I would let it play through the first chorus and maybe the second chorus if the crowd was feeling it but no longer. If you are familiar with this song, it starts with just Mariah Carey singing without instruments for the first several bars. I dropped this song in and watched the crowd's reaction. In all of my years DJing, I'd never seen a crowd react to a song like this. From the moment the first notes were sung by Mariah, the entire bar (200+ people) started screaming and yelling and subsequently sang the entire song word for word. It was one of the most amazing things I've witnessed as a DJ. It was as if nothing else mattered as we all enjoyed that one song. Truly amazing. I followed up this song with another popular song that was hot at the time. The rest of the night fed off the energy from the one Mariah Carey song. This is a perfect example of playing the right song at the right time and the impact it can have on an entire night.

The hardest part of playing at prime time in a club is keeping the crowd engaged for the entire 90-minute section. The perfect scenario is that you play hit after hit and everyone is fully engaged the entire time with no letdowns or drops in energy at all for 90 minutes. Based on my experience, this seemingly simple task is actually extremely difficult. Personally, there has been the rare occasion when I have been able to accomplish this, and it is a great feeling that is hard to top. The fact that it is rare and elusive continues to drive me to accomplish it again. I equate it to hitting for the cycle in baseball or scoring a hat trick in the World Cup against some of the best players in the world. It's possible but it isn't common.

My personal goal is to continue to chase these elusive 90-minute successes. Different people attending the club at different time periods with ever-changing song popularity make it like the greyhounds chasing the stuffed rabbit at a race. They almost catch it, but it never actually happens and so they keep chasing. The moment of truth for a DJ comes every night, usually around midnight. We can either continue to build the momentum or clear the dance floor and have to work the rest of the night to build it back up. One song can cause the dominoes to topple. We have to stay focused and follow the road the crowd leads us down. In business, there is always a time when the rubber meets the road and the company must perform and walk on its own legs.

Dallas

One of the most valuable lessons I learned in Dallas, Texas, as a general manager, was the preopening sales experience— launching a new brand in a city that had no knowledge of this brand, hiring a brand-new staff, and actually opening a brand-new business.

I fell in love with sales in the Lone Star State of Texas. Sales is the backbone of any business, and in order to be success- ful, you need to continue to grow sales and increase your client list as times evolve. I was tasked with opening up a new hotel with a small budget and high expectations. We were fortunate enough to have the strong brand presence behind our name.

To build a strong brand presence in any industry, there are no shortcuts. There is no magic advertisement, social media trick, or lead source you can purchase to get consistent, high-quality opportunities for business. You have to go out and meet people face to face and build relationships. A successful salesperson has authentic relationships with his or her customers so that referrals happen naturally and are a second thought to the relationship. The most effective referrals you can get in the business world are through word of mouth, and this will be the case until the end of time. It is as much as what you give in the relationship as what you receive.

What are the most popular venues in the local area that recommend DJs? Visit those venues and build a relationship with them. Get them to add you to their vendor list. What are the most popular clubs where you want to play? Visit these clubs and see what DJs play and what the style is on different nights.

In my DJ world, this would be the equivalent to talking to the DJs that are playing at a night in a club where we want to DJ and offering to collaborate with them. Nowadays, it is not about stealing that DJ's night but rather trying to work with them and figure out if there are any collaboration opportunities available. One of my first DJ mentors was DJ Tetris, who would play at a local bar in Hermosa Beach on Saturday nights. I would visit the bar, sit at the table closest to the DJ booth, and watch how he worked his way through the night. He would play different popular songs, blend them with new songs while scratching and beat juggling, and just having strong sets consistently week after week. Eventually, I got enough courage to ask him about his career, why he chose to play certain songs at certain times, and a little bit of business talk. Tetris was an open book with me, showed me how to properly use CDJs, and even worked with me and management to create one of my first monthly residencies at that same bar. I still apply the lessons I learned from Tetris to this day and I am forever grateful. This story came full circle, as I was able to invite him out to my Venice residency to guest DJ with me years later.

In the day and age we live in, we are always selling ourselves, our work, and our talents. No matter the business, we are always selling, and I am thankful I built such a strong sales foundation at such a young point in my life and career.

Seven Tips to Market Yourself as a DJ

There are many was to build your DJ brand and become well known around your region of the world. Here are seven tips that have helped me grow and develop my brand.

#1 – Create a website and social media platforms with all of the handles being uniform so that people can easily find and follow you. You will notice that if you follow me on social media, all of my handles are at @amaniexperience. This wasn't always the case, but as I evolved and learned how people prefer to find me, I made some adjustments and am now more uniform in my branding.

#2 – *Network with other DJs.* When you are new and trying to learn the ropes of the club and bar circuit, there is no more valuable resource than the DJs who have been around the area longer than you. They know who to talk to and who to avoid. Plus, the majority of my club leads and gigs have come from other DJs. I will also include networking via social media with other DJs. You can meet and get easy access to other DJs across social media. Drop a simple comment on their Instagram or Twitter about your seeing them at a local show. Authentic comments over a consistent time period will go a long way.

#3 – *Open up for other DJs.* A great way to build relationships with DJs in your area is to open up for them. This means that you will play the first hour to 90 minutes of their four-hour set. Be sure you know how to properly play an opening set (don't play any of the current hits or classic songs), and word will quickly spread that you are a collaborative DJ. As I mentioned before, my longest residency in my DJ career came from opening up for a fellow DJ friend and colleague and then having the club contact me directly to fill an open night. It works!

#4 – *Join a professional association as your DJ business and get involved.* One of the largest sources of leads for my DJ business has been due to my participation in the

Southern California Chapter of Meeting Professionals International (MPISCC). MPI is the largest meeting and event association worldwide that provides innovative and relative education, networking opportunities, and business exchanges. I recommend joining and then volunteering on a committee. What you give to the organization in terms of your time and knowledge, you will get back twofold. I jumped right in and am working my way up the leadership structure while learning and growing my business. This is the best of both worlds. Other similar associations that would be beneficial for DJs are SITE (Society of Incentive & Travel Executives), PCMA (Professional Convention Management Association), and ILEA (International Live Events Association).

#5 – *Visit clubs and bars you want to play in.* Make it a habit to visit the clubs and bars that you would like to play in on a regular basis. Say hello to the bartenders and security guards. Say hello to the DJs. Try to determine who the manager is and say hello. Don't go for a fast sell. Build a relationship while casually mentioning that you are a DJ and love the bar and the music they play. Consistently visit so that you become a regular and start the conversation about you playing a night there. Focus on the long game. You would be surprised how many times a potential gig may come up when you least expect it. Was the scheduled DJ a no-show? Did the bar manager forget to schedule a DJ? Always be ready.

#6 – *Invest time in online groups of DJs and creatives.* There is value in participating in online forums focused on the DJ community and the creative community. Active participation in private Facebook groups, Reddit subforums, Quora and LinkedIn groups can be fertile ground for learning, networking, and eventually a source for leads and referrals. I recommend spending 30 minutes each day answering questions, sharing opinions, giving out referrals, and reading through people's experiences and stories. I guarantee you will learn more than you expect, and you will meet other professionals on the same journey as you. Embrace these people as they are your tribe and will be there for you through the highs and lows.

#7 – Take a class. My DJ career took off when I enrolled in Scratch Academy in Los Angeles. I went to learn more skills and how to improve my DJ business. I ended up meeting great friends, learning a massive amount of information, and finding my tribe. Don't limit yourself to a DJ school. Maybe it is a class on social media, music theory, or comedy. Improv classes are great ways to meet similar creative artists, as DJs have to improvise every two minutes. The point is to learn and network at the same time. The personal development you will experience will increase your value.

As we finish off the peak time period of prime time, I have just run through a great medley of songs and then surprised the audience with a nice reggae throwback. Inhibitions are gone and the crowd is giving off amazing energy. People are exhausted and need a little break so they head to the bar for a quick refresh and I settle in for the final hour of the set. We are at the top of the mountain and now it is time for us to descend the mountain and cruise home safely.

The second prime-time moment in my career and life occurred when I moved to Los Angeles. Despite a massive amount of fear and uncertainty, I packed my bags and moved across the country. Two years later, we were in the midst of a serious economic downturn and my job was eliminated. I was fortunate enough to be rehired but I learned that it was important to diversify my income. Previously, I had put all my eggs in one basket and this was a major wakeup call. It was during this time when I swore to create some side income.

It was here in California that I summoned the courage to begin my DJ career, 13 years after declaring this is what I wanted to do when I grew up. People often ask me why I started DJing only once I moved to California. I always say that there is something about living in California, whether it be Silicon Valley up north or Hollywood in Southern California, that inspires you to go for your dreams. This is an intangible feeling I had compared to how I felt in the other places. The state encourages entrepreneurship, going for your dreams, and just taking risks. I caught the bug and was forever inspired when I landed here. The first step I took was to start a podcast (*The Mirth:Nadir Show*) where I would play love songs and dedications in addition to doing artist interviews. We had the opportunity to interview musicians such as Melanie Fiona, Donnell Jones, and Raheem Devaughn on the show. The show ran for three and a half years. In May of 2012, one of my closest friends told me about the world-renowned Scratch DJ Academy.

"Two points from passing is not good enough."

—DJ Hapa and DJ Revolution
(The Scratch DJ Academy, Los Angeles)

Scratch DJ Academy, Los Angeles

Although I was DJing at the time, I was self-taught with a few lessons from a friend. I needed to learn more so I signed up at Scratch Academy. I jumped in with both feet and immersed myself into becoming educated on my new career. It was a huge risk. Friends and family thought I was crazy.

"Is that a joke? What is a DJ school? Who goes to a DJ school?"

What they didn't realize was that this was 13 years in the making. By March of 2013, I had advanced through the entire curriculum of six classes, and it was time to find out if I had gotten my DJ certification. I ended up two points short of a passing grade. I was shocked. I was used to being a high achiever (general manager of a hotel at age 23, all-county soccer player, top salesperson with Marriott for three years in a row) and this was foreign territory.

This was also one of the best experiences for me to live through. In my podcast, I ask every one of my guests what their favorite failure is in life, and this experience is my answer to that question. It was at that very moment that I had to make a decision. Do I take my ball, go home, and let the previous nine months of work go to waste? Or do I swallow my pride, get my ego in check, and repeat the final class to improve my score?

1:00 A.M. – 1:15 A.M.

The Homestretch

....

"Music in the soul can be heard by the universe..."

— Lao Tzu

The 1:00 a.m. timeframe is like the top of the stretch run of a Triple Crown race. The jockey has done all the hard work navigating through a crowded field and positioned his or her horse to catch its stride at the right time down the homestretch. With a little luck, the horse has enough energy to pull away from the field and cruise home to a substantial victory. With the victory comes significant prizes, rewards, and adulation.

Once I get to 1:00 a.m. in the DJ booth, the hard work has been done. I've played most of the popular songs. Now I just have to string together a good 13 or 14 more songs to get us to 1:30 a.m. and the slow-down slow jam portion. The crowd is plenty warm (drunk). If I've done my job well, they love every song I play and we cruise home. I enjoy sneaking in some popular throwbacks as well as a few newer songs as the night winds down. People are usually losing energy at this point so I keep it as familiar as possible. I have also discovered that people are more apt to take dancing risks later in the night, which presents a perfect time to sneak in a salsa song or two to see what the crowd does with this genre The worst thing to do is to clear the floor at 1:15 a.m. with a full half hour of potential drinks going unsold. So I continue to connect the dots and string together a few more hits to bring it home.

Toward the end of the night, I like to play many of the random requests I have received throughout the night, as long as they fit in the general direction the music is going. If people have stayed this long patiently waiting for their requests, I feel obliged to reward their patience. This is like the customer care portion of business. You have the clients. Are they happy? Do they need anything else to keep them happy (a specific song)? It has been proven in business that it is more expensive to acquire a new customer than to keep a customer. During my sales career, this lesson was continuously emphasized as the relationships I maintained with clients allowed me to consistently book business across the country with past clients. Building relationships with club and bar attendees is very similar. If I give them what they want (to a degree), they will stay until last call and everyone wins.

Stability

In the business world, stability is like the calm water after a major storm. It often sneaks up on you and can last for an extended period of time if you manage all of the aspects of business at a consistent level. Quarterly dividends to stockholders, growth of revenues year over year, and low associate turnover are all positive signals that stability in your business has arrived. In general, there are minimal attempts to diverge from the current business operation and add any new services or products. In layman's terms, we want to ride this train as long as possible while keeping an eye on future trends so we can adjust if necessary. This stage offers all business owners a time to catch their breath and prepare for what is next in the business' lifetime while reaping their rewards for the previous years of hard work.

Within the DJ world, a set could be going along smoothly and then things can get hectic with multiple requests, demands from the bar owner, and an unpredictable crowd that is hard to read. As DJs, we have to fight through this and work our way through to a time period in our set when it gets calmer and things get back to normal. Usually, this time arrives as we move from the end of prime time to the end of the night. If we have had a good night and the crowd has been feeling every song we have played, we have experienced stability the whole night. Often, it has not been a smooth road and somehow, someway, we have survived and landed at this point in time. When flying on a plane, you will notice that right before you touch down, there is a time period when the pilot will cut the engines and you glide toward the ground. Stability for a DJ is this moment.

1:15 A.M. – 1:30 A.M.

Avoiding Distractions
and Staying Focused

....

"Starve your distractions, feed your focus."

—Tony Robbins

The list of distractions while DJing is a mile long. It can range from personal distractions to the most visual distractions. For example, it is 11:30 p.m., the club is crowded, and it hits you at this very moment that you forgot to go to the bathroom at the beginning of your set. Not only are you in the middle of a bunch of hit songs that are sure to keep the crowd primed but the line to the bathroom is very long. This is at least a seven- to eight-minute adventure if you are lucky. You can put on a very long song or what works better, play a prerecorded mix that gives you at least 15 minutes to make it happen. This whole bathroom dilemma reminds me of something that Z-Trip said to me once, "Go to the bathroom when you can, not when you have to!"

Or maybe you spot an attractive person at the club. I have to be honest and say that it can be quite distracting to catch a glimpse of an attractive female walking through the club or even walking toward me. The visual stimulation can cause you to pause as a DJ, and it usually happens right as you are preparing to mix in and out of a song. Staying focused takes a little bit of effort but it can be done. What is even worse is if you see the attractive female walking towards the DJ booth with eyes on you. It's sort of like those scenes of a movie when a man catches the eye of a woman and they are looking at each other for an extended amount of time until the man either runs into a wall or pole or just trips. I specifically recall one time a young woman approached the DJ booth, came around to the side of the booth, and just smiled and looked at me for at least 30 seconds. I smiled back and asked her how she was doing. Then she asked me for a favor, "Can I do some *yayo* (cocaine) on the turntables and take a picture or video?" She kept a straight face with a pretty smile and just looked at me expecting me to say yes. The only way I thought to respond was to first ask her to repeat what she said because I couldn't have heard her correctly. After she repeated the same request, the only way for me to respond after a pregnant pause and nervous laughter was to say, "I don't think that is a good idea." Out of nowhere came a friend of hers who quickly whisked her far away from the DJ booth. I can't lie. The whole rest of the night, I watched this woman to see what she would try to do in the public eye. A simple distraction threw me off for the entire night.

Other distractions include drunk people falling or making fools of themselves, people trying to get my attention for requests, and then continuing to ask (or in some cases demand) that I play their song before they leave. Why would I play your song if you were about to leave? The drunk-people-falling distraction is a tough one because I want everyone to be safe and enjoy the club, but if someone is putting themselves in danger, I do have a responsibility to make sure they get to safety. Normally, there is a security guard near the DJ booth whom I can alert when someone needs help immediately. If there is not a security guard there, I can signal to the bar (using the light from my cell phone) or actually run from the DJ booth to grab the closest security guard. Although my top priority is keeping the party going by playing the hits, I also must partner with the club or bar to make sure we have a safe environment. Plus, my hospitality background causes me to be extra diligent as I am DJing.

Frequently, celebrities might even enter the club. They might come up to the booth and give you props, make a request, stay in VIP and send their people up to you to make requests, or just stay anonymous and not approach you at all. One time, I was DJing a party for Samuel L. Jackson's agent in Marina del Rey, and he came up to me and gave me props. You still have to stay focused and play for everyone else in the club.

The equivalent to distraction in business is the shiny thing example of prophecy. In business, there are many things that will catch your eye and distract you from your mission or purpose. The shiny things will catch your eyes but end up having little to no depth. As you get more experienced in the business world, you learn how to avoid the temptation that shiny objects bring to you and stay focused.

Many times, it could be the thought of a new product or service offering that could potentially bring in more revenue. Other times, it could come in the form of a friend or business colleague using the infamous phrase, "Why don't you do this?" Suggesting an improvement to the business or a new service to offer can be tempting, but the most successful businesses niche down as much as possible until it is obvious that an addition to the business would help. It could be the perfect space becoming available for new office space when you are just fine in the office space you currently occupy. Distractions can come in many ways and are often not recognized until too late. This is where self-awareness and a laser focus on what is important to the mission will lessen the impact of distractions on your daily job.

1:30 A.M. – 1:45 A.M.

Time for Slow Jams!

....

"Memory is the diary that we all carry about us."
—*Oscar Wilde*

Radio Love Song Dedications

Silver Spring, Maryland, May 1991

I am listening to the radio and hear a song dedication from a girl to a boy of the song "A Ribbon in the Sky" by Stevie Wonder. I change the station during the next commercial and hear a boy declare his love and dedicate Extreme's "More Than Words" to her. I think to myself, "I want to be the DJ they call for the love song dedications. I want to help them get the boy or girl to fall in love with them."

Since the fifth or sixth grade, I have been passionate about love songs and the moments it can create between two people. I credit this unique interest for a fifth grader to two factors. First, I loved listening to Quiet Storm radio shows at nighttime when the dedications would come in from around the Washington, DC area. The skill of listening to a person's request and being able to quickly identify the right song to play in the moment was one that I yearned to

emulate from the DJs who were on the radio as I was growing up. Second, I was a huge fan of John Hughes growing
up, and every one of his movies had a signature love song
at a pivotal moment in the movie. The fact that in many
instances the love song would become a bigger hit than the
actual movie was further confirmation. The combination of
these two factors had me hooked on love songs for life!

I began to hone my mixtape skills during my high school
and college days and loved to put together slow jam
mixtapes for all the women in whom I was interested. I
continued that practice throughout my young adult life. It
has now evolved to live mixes with turntables, mixers, and
pressure. I still love it.

Why do I love the last 15-20 minutes of DJing at a club?
The people who stay at a club or bar to the very end either want to party until the last song or they are trying to
close the deal with a person they met earlier in the night.
Whichever category you fall into, I am there to help you
enjoy. This is when I can be even more creative.

I love playing a few slow jams to encourage old-school slow
dancing and people singing along to their favorite love
songs. A hidden benefit of doing this exercise as the night
is coming to a close is that it allows me to finish strong,
because I never want to finish a gig with less energy, desire,
or attention to detail as when the gig began. I owe it to the
people who are still at the club at 1:35 a.m. to give them the
maximum amount of energy and care. I never know who
is in the crowd and who might be watching the DJ all the

way until the very end. I try to be just as focused on mixing and picking the right song at 1:35 a.m. as I am at 11:30 p.m. By this time, people are quite drunk. I have found that slow songs that bring back memories of high school or even middle school work the best during this time because of nostalgia. Of course, I'll have to analyze the perceived average age group of the crowd and do the math.

Thinking back, if you put on a popular love song from the late 1980s, my memories would immediately go back to a seventh-grade dance at Takoma Park Middle School. If you put on one of Whitney Houston's slow jam hits from 1991-1992, I would be transported back to my high school prom. The list of songs and memories paired with each song could go on forever. If you look at Usher's run of hits in the early 2000s, you would find several top 10 hits that are slow jams. This means that most young adults of today were in middle school, high school, or just beginning college then, and the memories these different songs trigger would be fresh and nostalgic in a good or bad way. People know the words from songs of their youth, and they sing along to the entire song. I have numerous go-to slow jams, depending on the age breakdown of the crowd that I am playing for. The goal at the end of the night is to play a set of songs that leaves the crowd begging for more. At times, I will sneak in some current slow jams that have taken the music world by storm. Even for current slow songs, people have stopped what they were doing and started singing along word for word while swaying to the music. That type of musical experience fills up my cup!

By the time we get to 1:30, I have been DJing for three and a half hours and I'm starting to get tired. I try to keep the energy high and finish the night out strong. Playing some slow jams and seeing the crowd's reaction gives me energy to experiment and try new things.

One of the best feelings at the end of the night (besides sitting down after four to five hours on my feet) is when the crowd is ambivalent (in a good way) about hearing one more song. That means you did your job perfectly and the patrons should leave very pleased. Standing ovations are not common in the DJ world, especially for up-and-coming DJs. I can recall one time when I was in the flow and strung together about six to seven songs at the perfect time at the end of the night, and when the lights came on and the music went off, the crowd just stopped and clapped for me. It was an amazing feeling and has only happened one time (so far) in my career. Job well done, I would say.

Nostalgia in Business

If you have a product or service and you can somehow bring positive nostalgia into the marketing or branding, it will help you increase the demographics of the people you can reach.

The term "nostalgia" was first coined in the seventeenth century by a Swiss physician, Johannes Hofer, who attribut-ed soldiers' mental and physical afflictions to their longing to return home. Initially, nostalgia had a negative connota-tion, such as "a neurological disease of essentially demonic cause," "immigrant psychosis," or "a mentally repressive compulsive disorder." As research on nostalgia has increased in recent years, the views on the subject have undergone a radical shift. Most people experience nostalgia once a week, while nearly half the population experiences nostalgia three to four times a week. Once evoked, nostalgia reestablishes psychological equanimity, elevates mood, improves self-esteem, and gives a sense of social connectedness. It increases meaning in life and fights off death cognitions. A favorite tool of researchers to spark nostalgia is music. Studies have proven that music has actually caused people to feel warmer when experiencing nostalgia![13] [14]

> *"Nostalgia brings to mind cherished experiences that assure us we are valued people who have meaningful lives. Some of our research shows that people who regularly engage in nostalgia are better at coping with concerns about death."*
>
> —*Dr. Clay Routledge (North Dakota State University)*

Neuroimaging has shown that songs stimulate many different areas of the brain and give a bit of a dopamine high

---

13 Tierney, John, "What Is Nostalgia Good For ? Quite a Bit, Research Shows," *The New York Times*,. July 8, 2013. https://www.nytimes.com/2013/07/09/science/what-is-nostalgia-good-for-quite-a-bit-research-shows.html.

14 University of Southampton Nostalgia Group. "Nostalgia." University of Southampton. Accessed July 23, 2019. https://www.southampton.ac.uk/nostalgia/.

while they are playing. If I can give someone a legal high by playing some slow jams, I am all for it.

At Marriott, we would use photos of old Marriott hotels or root beer stands from back in the day. These simple photos had a masterful impact on educating old and young guests on the history of the company. Other companies have old advertisements or commercials playing in their corporate lobbies or on their YouTube channel that serve as nostalgia marketing. Some companies will use a mixture of old and new footage in their videos to bridge the gap. I feel this is a valuable way to reach different demographics and attract new clients. People love to think back to their youth as a time of less stress, no burdens, no bills, and a more freeing and unrestricted feeling. Look at the success that ESPN Classic has. They show classic games of all sports and you have to answer the question, "Where were you when this game was happening?" Nostalgia is a powerful emotion. If a standing ovation comes with the trip down memory lane, then you know you have struck the right nerves. This is the goal of the end-of-night, slow-jam exercise. I love it.

OMG, He Came Back!

As I finish up with the final slow jam and the crowd is beginning to disperse, the agent whom I saw leave the club earlier comes from out of nowhere and has a group of four other people with him. He tells me, "I left to go get them from another bar and bring them here. The vibe and music were much better over here and I wanted to expose them to your style. Tremendous job tonight. I love how you played all of the current hits but also took us on a journey back to our younger days by playing some great throwbacks. That was fun! I will definitely be in touch real soon as I want to get you out at some of my spots on a Friday, Saturday, or Sunday night. I appreciate your style and think our crowds would love you." This was an actual booking agent who continues to book me monthly at different venues across Southern California.

With that, he shakes my hand, as do the rest of his party, and they head out the door. I smile to myself and think about how I was worried and temporarily heartbroken for nothing.

> *"Worry gives a small thing a big shadow."*
>
> *—Swedish proverb*

1:45 A.M. – 2:00 A.M.

The Night Is Over

....

*"You don't have to go home, but you have to
get the hell out of here."*

—*Anonymous*

The night is complete. You finish the last song and people begin their mass exodus from the club. I enjoy watching people as they leave. Many of the patrons are intoxicated and staggering out of the club. We make sure they hop in an Uber, a Lyft, or a cab. Often, people will come by and say, "Thank you" or "Nice job!" There have been a few times when people have said, "You didn't play [this song] or [that song]." Over the years, I've learned that feedback is a gift. I have learned to not get too high when receiving compliments and not to get too low when receiving criticism. I do my best to keep my feet on the ground, as my DJ teacher and mentor has told me several times.

Uber Confessionals

Sometimes, I drive for Uber on my way home from the club. I try to find someone going my direction and take them home to earn a little money from the trip. Gas money comes in many forms and a little bit here and there will always help. I prefer to pick up people from the club where I just worked, take them home, and get feedback on the night.

One time, I picked up a group of women and they were so happy and excited from the night they had had. I asked them how they enjoyed the night and they raved about the music and dancing and the fun they had had. When I told them that I was the DJ that night, they paused for maybe five seconds before they started to scream and were very, very complimentary. It was funny and I can't lie, it did make me feel good. Another time, I picked up a man and drove him back home. I asked him about the night. He was lukewarm and said that he wished the DJ would have played more songs to get the women on the dance floor and keep them there. He even said he was expecting to hear a particular song. I told him I was the DJ and I appreciated the feedback. He was surprised at first, but then we got into a great discussion about different songs I played or didn't play and my thought behind it. Based on his feedback, I adjusted the type of songs I played the next week at the club to see what might change with the women on the dance floor. Sure enough, he had a point, and when I played songs from artists like Cassie, Lauryn Hill, and Beyoncé, the reaction was a stream of women going to the dance floor and plenty of singing along. I now keep these songs by these artists as part of my regular rotation and mix them in, as well as add newer songs to the list.

Every successful business will seek out feedback about

their products or services from their customers. In some instances, focus groups are also a common and effective way of learning what is working well and what needs to be improved. Although, technically, my Uber experience is outside of the 10:01 p.m. to 2:00 a.m. time period, I find the feedback valuable and I still use this technique to this day. I view the various rides I give as my mini focus groups. Businesses should always seek feedback and find ways to improve customer and client expectations.

Back to the club. After everyone is done, I will check with security to make sure everything went well and ask if they had any concerns. Were there too many people near the DJ booth? Did any songs cause any fights or general rowdiness from the crowd? At the end of the night, were we able to clear the club in a prompt and effective manner? My final stop is to check with the bartender and the manager to see how the night went. Sometimes, they will be appreciative that I played a favorite song of theirs. Other times, they will comment on a string of songs I played that were too predictable. Generally, the bartenders are happy after a night when I have kept the club busy and was able to cycle through the dance floor and ensure that people continued to have their tabs open and bought drinks. Most of the time, the manager is happy and pleased with how the night went.

Don't Go Too Hard Too Soon (Thanks V-Fresh!)

I recall one time I was at one of my residencies and it was around 11:05 p.m. I was in a bit of a mood that evening. During the set, I went too hard too soon (did not make a good transition from older, more recognizable songs to current hits) in the night, and some of the locals closed out their tabs and left earlier than usual. The manager made a beeline to the DJ booth and expressed his displeasure. I learned to pay closer attention to the crowd when I arrived to ensure that the bar guests who were already there and vibing with the mood stayed while I also worked to lure people in from outside.

This is a difference of DJing at a bar compared to a club. At a club, people will pay an entrance fee to get in, and you usually have a captured audience for at least two to three hours. It is rare for people to pay an entrance fee and then leave soon after. Inside of a club, there are various VIP sections and pockets of regulars who can be quite demanding on the DJ. You must learn to balance their requests with the general flow of the night. At a bar, there is usually free entrance so people are coming and going throughout the night. I have learned that the key is to make a seamless transition from the guests who are at the bar when you start (10:00 p.m.) to the rest of the general patrons who arrive around 11:00 to 11:30 p.m. The managers of the bar love to keep the after-dinner guests in the bar for as long as possible, while having music that is universal enough to draw people in from the outside and get them to open up tabs and stay. It keeps the bar manager happy, and the patrons who are around earlier in the night will stay and spend more money on drinks, keeping the bar full. This is a delicate balance that has taken years of practice to master.

This experience with the manager getting upset taught me to adjust my DJ strategy and read the room better in these instances. You can be assured that the manager of this bar has never had to worry about me chasing patrons out of the bar too soon ever again. The challenge comes when it's time to segue from the classic throwback songs to more current music. We don't want the guests who have just arrived to turn right back around and leave, yet we are trying to squeeze as much time as possible from the people who are already in the bar. I compare this to trying to please two bosses at the same time. In my experience, what has worked well is to slowly shift to more popular hits from the '80s and '90s while mixing in a bit of new music. Each song will touch on what the different demographics in the club or bar want to hear and in many cases appeal to all the people there. From here, I would continue on and use this same strategy until eventually I can completely focus on more current hits from the last five years. This does not mean I will dismiss entirely the original patrons who were at the bar from the beginning. I love to sneak in a classic song in the middle of more current hits in order to not be as predictable in the songs and the order of songs I am playing. A fun strategy I use when possible is to play the original of a song and then the current version of a song that is using a sample. A DJ's role has shifted from educating people about music to being a music curator, but these small educational lessons are always fun to share and play out. I continue to add to this list, and it is fun to add newer songs to this list.

In business, we must be able to meet the needs of many customers of different backgrounds all at the same time and make these customers feel like they are the top priority at all times. Playing different genres of music while moving through the night and keeping as many people in the bar or club as engaged as possible is a great example of this.

The day after my sets, I find myself hearing songs or thinking of songs and saying to myself, "I forgot to play that last night." I have learned that I can never play every song I planned on playing. It never fails that a very popular song will slip by me and I only realize it the next morning. I add this song to a list in my notebook and crates within Serato and make sure I play it the next set I have.

Basic DJ Definitions

Below is a list of basic DJ terminology that will help you continue to understand the terms used in this book.

DJ – The common definition for DJ is the individual who controls the music at an event by selecting songs and mixing them together using turntables, a controller, CDJs or any type of mixer. DJs include radio DJs, video DJs (they play the music videos of the songs along with the music), party DJs, corporate DJs, and wedding DJs. DJs must be able to select the proper songs at the correct time and use the order in which they play each song as a way of telling a story.

BPM – Beats Per Minute. How fast the rhythm of a song is going per minute. The faster the song, the higher the BPM. The slower the song, the lower the BPM.

Mixing – When a DJ transitions from one song to another song through proper beatmatching, scratching, or the judicious use of effects.

Remix – When a DJ or music producer changes the entire feel, tempo, and vibe of a song through the addition (or subtraction) of musical instruments, special effects, vocals, and other harmonic/melodic additions. Official remixes are through agreements with the record company or via remix contests.

Mashup – Two songs that are played together in a musical production. Most times, the instrumental of one track is playing along with the acapella of another track. Z-Trip is known as the godfather of the "mashup movement."

Bootleg – An unofficial and unlicensed remix or version of a song. Oftentimes, bootleg versions of songs are better than the originals.

Bar – In the DJ world with the 4/4 time signature, a bar is considered four (4) head nods or four beats.

Balancing Levels – Using the overall master volume along with the individual volume of the track (gain) that is playing to normalize the volume coming out of the main speakers. This is crucial when playing songs that are recorded at different volumes.

Bass – The low end of the song that is playing. The thump.

Bassline – This is the foundation for any song in dance music, and it's produced by the bass.

Beat Matching – The process of mixing two songs together by matching the speed (tempo), instrumentation, and pitch of both songs seamlessly at the proper time of the song (chorus, intro, outro, break, bridge).

Break – A portion of the song where the singing usually stops, the tempo changes, or there are only instrumentals playing. Break dancers commonly used breaks in songs for performances and battles back in the day.

CDJ – A CD player that allows analog control of music playing from CDs, usually using a recreation of a typical vinyl turntable.

Chorus – The part of a song with vocals that is typically repeated a few times at the beginning, middle, and end of a song. Frequently, this is the most popular portion of the song and lends itself to be sung along with the audience. This portion of the song is also called the hook and is a proper mix point when beatmatching.

Controller – Controllers are portable units that allow DJs to perform without having a large setup of CDJs or turntables. Controllers can also be used as mixers with turntables or CDJs attached to them. The major brands that currently have controllers are Pioneer, Denton, Numark, and others.

Copyright – Per Webster, copyright is the exclusive legal right, given to an originator or an assignee to print, publish, perform, film, or record literary, artistic, or musical material, and to authorize others to do the same.

Cross-fader – This feature on mixers and controllers allows the DJ to fade between two songs by simply moving the element to the left or right.

Cue – This is a visual marker that signals to the DJ the proper starting point to mix in or out of a song.

Cut – The act of scratching to introduce another song or scratching while a song is playing.

Deck – The primary device that has music on it via a CDJ or turntable.

Digital Vinyl System (DVS) – This invention from the early 2000s allows DJs to use individual music on computer files as a replacement for actual vinyl records or CDJs through computers or USB drives. The primary example of this is Serato DJ.

Edit – A revised version of a song that allows for extra elements within the song such as extended intros, outros, breaks, double choruses, or additional verses. Many DJs make their own edits.

EQ – The controls on a mixer that allow the DJ to adjust the highs (trebles), mids, and low (bass) frequencies of a specific song to harmonically blend the two songs together for optimal mixing.

Fader – A control on the mixer that allows the DJ to increase or decrease the volume of a song smoothly.

FX – Also known as "effects." These controls allow the DJ to manipulate the sounds of the current song in multiple ways include:

- **Flanger** – An audio effect that is produced when the output signal is usually fed back to the input (a "recirculating delay line") producing a resonance effect which further enhances the intensity of the peaks and troughs.

- **Phaser** – This is a popular effect that creates a sweeping effect on the song which is similar to a riser in music production.

- **Gain** – This allows the DJ to increase or reduce the volume of a specific song that is playing while not adjusting the master volume level.

- **Echo** – This special effect adds an echo to the track that is currently playing.

- **Delay** – This effect creates an auditory illusion that the same track is playing twice, one slightly behind the other track. This is also known as a more consistent sounding echo with no stop.

- **Reverb** – This effect gives the song that is playing a sound that is similar to when a sound hits any hard surface and reflects back to the listener at varying times and amplitudes to create a complex echo.

Juggle – Also known as beat juggling. This is a technique used by turntablists to the same song and creates an entirely different song by alternating back and forth between each song at specific points of the song, all while remaining on the beat and in the flow of the music that is playing. This is one of the more creative skills a turntablist can exemplify.

Looping – This a function that allows the DJ to play a certain part of a song over again repeatedly without stopping. The time signature can be as short as a 1/32 note or as long as 16 bars of the song.

Headphone Monitor – This is also known as the headphone cue and allows the DJ to hear what song is playing on a specific deck connected to the mixer.

Hook – Synonymous with the chorus, this is often the most recognizable part of a song and occurs at the beginning, middle, and end of a song. Many times, this is the preferred portion of the song that an audience will sing along to.

Intro – The beginning of a song, before any verses or choruses have occurred. Many DJs use the intro to mix into the next song.

Loop – Any part of a song that you repeat. This can often become the gateway to a new song or the part that you use to beat match.

Low – The bass portion of a song or the bottom end of the frequency spectrum. The rumble is a common slang for this.

High – The highest part of the frequency spectrum where the majority of high hats, shakers, rides, and keys are. Female vocals also commonly live in this space.

Mids – The portion of a song where within the frequency range where the snares, claps, and synths usually reside. Many male vocals also live in this space.

MP3 – This is a common digital format for music that many DJs use in place of vinyl records and CDJs. This music is downloaded to a computer or USB drive and then used to mix music together.

Outro – This portion of a song occurs after the final chorus, bridge, or verse and signals the end of a song. This is also a proper mixing point of a song.

Phrase – Any bit of music you can hear repeating during a song; normally each instrument has its own phrase, the drums do a beat, the bass does a bass line, etc. Each repeats the same thing during the chorus or verse but may change in the break/middle 8.

Rig – A term among mobile DJs that include the entire DJ setup including speakers, subwoofers, turntables/CDJs/controller), microphone, and computer.

1s and 2s – Slang name for turntables.

Wheels of Steel – Slang name for turntables that was first coined in the early 1970s by the first DJs in New York City.

Mapping Out a Song

This preparation technique is not discussed frequently in DJ circles, but I feel that it is crucial to your success in any type of gig you perform. Simply put, mapping out a song is writing down (or inserting markers in every song) how many bars the intro, verse, chorus, bridge, and outro are in a specific song. This teaches students the proper places to mix in and out of songs and the patterns of song structure. For example, one song you are playing may have a 12-bar intro, each chorus has 16 bars, there is an 8-bar bridge in the middle of the song, and the outro is 16 bars. You would put markers inside of the DJ software (Serato, Traktor, Rekordbox, etc.), which would give you a visual cue of what part of the song is coming up and how long the specific part lasts. Then, as you play the song and prepare to mix in the next song, you know how long you have to mix in and out. In this example, you would have 16 bars of a chorus to mix in and out of or the 8-bar bridge to mix into, unless you want to wait for the entire song and then mix in during the outro.

As a bonus, if you had a song that started with vocals, you could use the 8-bar bridge to mix in and out of the vocals and it would sound good. We live by a general rule of "no vocals over vocals," and the mapping helps us see where our opportunities are. Similar to driving a car a long distance when you don't know exactly how you are going to get to your final destination, you need a map to show you how to get there. In a DJ set, you know you need to start with the first song at 10:01 p.m. and end with the final song at 1:45 a.m. but you don't know how you will get there. The individual mapping will help you get from song to song and be as confident and assured as possible.

During a typical DJ set, you can play over 120 different songs, and I have found that it is best to have a roadmap for each one. Every time I teach this concept to my DJ students, my mapping skills get a little sharper, as does my ability to recognize song structures and analyze different patterns on the fly. I also teach students how to beat match. This crucial skill can be the most difficult to learn but also the most rewarding as you see people experience the proper way to blend two songs together. Breaking down the individual steps required with this process helps me hone my own skills and improve my ears, major and minor adjustments. Learning this skill requires a good amount of patience, which is a tertiary virtue in building opportunities that happen during the teaching process.

As the famous singer Phil Collins once said, "*In learning you will teach, and in teaching you will learn.*" Very true words.

2:00 A.M. – 2:30 A.M.

Self-Care

....

*"If your compassion does not include yourself,
it is incomplete."*

—*Jack Kornfield*

Self-care is crucially important. This can mean anything from wearing the proper shoes to the more complex issues around mental health, drug use, and alcohol. At times, the issues stem from having the proper type of healthcare so you can see a doctor. In my experience, it has been a journey to properly manage self-care and continue to be clear-headed and present as much as possible on a daily basis. Late nights with a generous amount of temptation can be a vicious combination to work through as you try to ascend within the industry.

I have witnessed DJ colleagues fall victim to a variety of vices that have ultimately led to their death. The most significant example that is still front of mind today is the story of DJ AM. DJ AM was a supremely talented DJ who came up playing private parties for his friends and then an unlicensed club in Los Angeles. His career continued to flourish as he expanded into Hollywood and then the biggest clubs in Vegas. DJ AM had a unique style of combining different genres, wordplay, scratching, impeccable mixing, a deep catalogue of musical knowledge, and perfect timing to literally leave crowds amazed as they witnessed his performances. He was well ahead of his time and grew to be one of the biggest DJs in the world during the first decade of the 2000s. Unfortunately, he could never fully overcome a drug addiction that had been an issue in his life for many years. DJ AM passed away in August 2009 from what doctors described as acute intoxication from a variety of drugs. His death was mourned by DJs worldwide and served as a reminder for all of us to take care of each other as tomorrow is not guaranteed.

In terms of eating healthy and filling your body up with the best possible fuel, I have witnessed many peers with phenomenal habits around eating and hydrating before, during, and after a gig. For the basic four-hour set starting at 10:00 p.m., the best time to eat a meal would be at 8:00 p.m. so that your energy level remains high throughout the entire time of your set, yet you will not feel heavy, bloated, or weighed down during your set. I also recommend drinking your fair share of water before the set and making one final stop in the bathroom at least 15 minutes before you start your set. I can't remember how many times I have had to get to the bathroom during a set and had to deal with a crowd on the way there and back. My female DJ colleagues have it even worse, as many times they have to fight a line once they reach the bathroom. Thank goodness for security guards who are available to escort them to the bathroom.

It has been my practice to avoid drinking at all during my gigs. I may have a light drink (Malibu and pineapple) before my set starts, but once it begins, I will rotate between water, cranberry juice, and ginger ale depending on how I feel throughout the night. Being clear-headed and alert is my primary goal throughout the entire time I am inside the club.

The past few years, we have seen an uptick in violence inside clubs, and I need to be prepared to handle any emergencies that arise throughout the night. I refuse to let fear prevent me from working at clubs and bars, but I do want to make sure I am always alert enough to protect myself as best as possible. My personal policy is the same regarding illicit drugs of any type. I don't even smoke weed before, during, or after sets so that my paranoia doesn't take over and I am uber-focused on being as clear-headed as possible.

A Strong Tribe

Only fellow DJs can relate to the long nights, rude customers, difficult bar owners, and the other various challenges we face on a weekly basis. I cannot emphasize this enough as we cannot thrive in this business alone. One of my favorite sayings is from an African proverb that states, "If you want to go fast, go alone. If you want to go far, go together."

I have numerous DJ colleagues in my tribe (Kurtis Cross, DJ Dazzler, V Fresh, Eli M, Tina T, DJ Tessa, DJ Ivy, Bella Fiasco, DJ Michael Basic, DJ Slyde, As-Is, and so many more to name) that allow me to have a safe space to discuss issues, ask questions, seek advice, and sometimes just vent about that crazy club or bar manager I have to deal with on a weekly basis. Despite the fact that we perform in front of large crowds for many of our gigs, DJing can be a very lonely world. We operate in a silo during all of our gigs and usually have few people to chat with during our gigs besides security and perhaps an opening or closing DJ.

After DJing for a few years, inevitably we experience a rut or a creative slump. Generally, playing the same set of songs (which is required to please the public's expectations) can wear on you, as the most creative gigs are few and far between. Fighting through these creative ruts is tough and can put you in a dark place. I know a few DJ colleagues who have had to walk away for years at a time just to break out of the slump and refill their metaphorical cup. To refill my own cup, I schedule time to watch other DJs when they come to town and attend regular music shows as a guest. It is good to observe what other DJs do as they navigate the night and use the music to tell a story.

I also do music swap with other DJs. Many times, I will hear new songs or different versions of songs and that is all it takes to break out of the slump. I also recommend developing a strong group (think of a mastermind) of DJs to meet with monthly and just share what you're going through. I find we all go through similar feelings and ex-periences no matter if we are playing in front of crowds of 50 people or 50,000 people. It is all relative. This is a best practice that I will continue to follow as my career expands.

Life Doesn't Happen to You, It Happens for You (A Lesson)

A few years ago, I was working at a club every week on Friday nights and things were going very well. The club was busy on my specific night. Alcohol sales were great, and I had regulars who came only when I was DJing. A new manager came into the club and wanted to make some changes. Within one week, I was no longer the only DJ on Friday nights. I had to submit my availability and wait to see which days I got booked. Initially, my ego ran amuck, and I was furious, confused, and distraught.

I didn't understand.

I was fortunate to have other DJ friends I could talk to. One of my DJ friends advised me to look at this situation from a different perspective. Instead of thinking about the dates and cache I was losing at the club, I should look it as an opportunity to rest on some Friday nights while opening myself up for additional opportunities for different gigs across the city. It was a chance to build on my reputation outside that one club. She also encouraged me to check my ego and realize perhaps I need to improve my skills so that eliminating my nights would be more difficult for a different club in the future.

Receiving feedback or tough love is very difficult at times. I find it even more difficult when it comes from friends who know you the best. However, this form of feedback was important for my self-care, as it prevented me from taking this issue personally and opened my mind to future possibilities that were better. Many times, a simple issue like our ego can ruin our progress if we don't have the necessary self-care to work through it. I view this as a minor occurrence in my career but a major lesson.

In addition, I encourage people to open up their circle of influence and include other creatives as well. I have found immense value in consistent discussions with creatives who work in photography, event planning, graphic design, singing, writing, acting, and other spaces. This creative journey is a grind and can weigh on you. Having a strong tribe of people around me at all times has helped me not slip into the common rabbit holes of depression, self-doubt, the comparison trap, and feelings of inadequacy. We cannot discount the fact that as creatives, we are always putting ourselves out there when we perform or when we attempt to book new business. The most common thing we hear is "no." and we have to have the mental resilience to keep pushing forward with the thought that this specific "no" puts us closer to our next "yes."

We need the proper level of self-care so that a setback does not paralyze us. I also feel that having the proper people around us will inspire us to get out of our comfort zones and look to grow. It does the heart good to see yourself growing professionally. More so than earning a lot of money, if we are growing, learning, and improving, we will be happier and more productive and will continue to push ourselves outside of our comfort zones. This is a crucial part of self-care.

The most valuable philosophy that I learned while working for Marriott that is still in the soul of the company today is, "If you take care of the associates, they will take care of the guests, and the guests will be happy." Many other companies before and after Marriott was created have used this strategy of making sure they take the best care of their employees so that they love to come to work and will even spend extra time at work taking care of their clients. Taking this mindset further, a guest I interviewed on my podcast said, "None of this works if you don't work," and this is a profound statement. I have learned that mental health days are real things. Staycations can be more valuable than traditional vacations. The businesses that take care of their associates and encourage their associates to take care of themselves will continue to perform at the highest levels.

3:00 A.M.

Reflections

*"Life can only be understood backwards
but must be lived forwards."*

—*Soren Kierkegaard*

The night is over and it is time for bed. The goal is to get eight hours of sleep and repeat the process tomorrow for my next gig. As I settle into bed, I think about songs I should have played throughout the night. I put the notebook on my nightstand to good use as I write notes before I drift off to sleep.

I do take a minute to acknowledge how fortunate I am to have the career that I have. It has been quite a journey from starting as a bellman at the Washington West End Marriott to writing a book about how the times of a DJ set relates to the stages of a business. I wonder if I will fall asleep right away or will my mind continue to wander.

The Climax of the Scratch DJ Academy LA Experience

It all starts at Woodlin Elementary School, where I am known as DJ Fresh. I participate in the school talent show as the DJ in a breakdancing crew. We win first place. They don't let me dance a solo during the show. I am so upset I cry and swear that I will redeem myself for that omission. I subconsciously commit to becoming a DJ when I grow up.

Now years later in another school, I'm trying to pass the Scratch Academy DJ certification program. Many nights I think back to the crucial time period when I was sitting in that room in Scratch Academy and heard the words from DJ Hapa and DJ Revolution that I was not good enough to graduate. I failed Mixing 505.

The worst part of that specific day is that we had an alumni and certification student mixer where past alumni would come back and speak to members of the certification program about life after DJ school and offer tips and advice in terms of what we should do to grow our careers.

I can think back to no other moment in my life being so humbling. The day is quite clear in my mind. I had to drive home down the 405 to walk my dog and then back to the school while dealing with the second-lowest feeling of my life (the first was when my dad passed away suddenly). Let's not even talk about the fact the young woman I was trying to date completely dissed me that same week! To be in the same room with my classmates who *did* pass as everyone

knew I didn't was awful. I frequently refer back to that moment as a turning point in my DJ career as well as my life.

There is no exaggeration when I say that. I came to a specific point in my career when I could have basically quit and
refused to fight through the pain and embarrassment of not
passing.

I made the decision to repeat the final class and ask for help.
I needed to rebuild my mixing and beat-matching foundation so I signed up for additional lessons. This is where I was
able to work one on one with V Fresh, which was the true
beginning of our friendship and future music production
partnership. I bought a set of turntables and a basic Numark
two-channel mixer and would practice at night in my living
room. I had to basically relearn how to mix, starting with
working with hip-hop instrumentals and mixing them from
a low bpm up to a high bpm. From there, I then had to relearn the proper points in the song to mix in and out of and
perfect my timing. Despite the humbling feeling of being
a beginner and the feeling of regression, I fought through
the pain and began to strengthen my fundamentals. As the
lessons continued, it was if something finally clicked and
I was able to take a huge step in the development of my
DJ skills. I recognized my need for assistance and asked for
help. I was open to feedback and focused on getting better.

As the beginning of the final class (part two) approached, I
have to be clear and say that there was no guarantee that I
would pass the second class just because I was repeating it.

It would take more hard work, focus, determination, and humility.

I had made it through all the weekly classes, and my total class score was very high. But like always, it comes down to the final exam. There have been many people who have had higher scores than me heading into the final and have still failed the class.

I remember going up to Scratch Academy on Saturday afternoons and practicing with my classmates as we all were preparing for each exam. We would drill each other on the exercises and work on our potential sets. It was a special time in my DJ career and life, though I did not realize the level of growth I was going through personally and professionally.

For the final exam, the person with the highest score in the class could choose in what order they would like to perform for the final exam. The first time I went through the exam, I was 17 out of 24 students. This next time through the class, I had earned the opportunity to choose my time first. I chose to go first out of 25 students. Once again, we were simulating the time period of a club. In real life it was 10:00 a.m. on a Sunday, but for the final exam, it was 10:00 p.m. on a Saturday night. I was inside setting up to DJ with no one else in the club as it had not "opened" yet. I was nervous only until I was able to get sound up on both sides (both turntables) and then I was off and running. I played "Mary Jane" by Rick James as part of my opening set. That song now has special meaning to me more than what Rick James is discussing in the song.

After waiting through 24 other performances that were all over the map, with emotions running high the entire class, it was over. The instructors had us wait for almost an hour as they debated on who would pass the class or who would fail the class, needing to repeat (if they chose). I was pretty confident I had passed but there was no guarantee. This time, they called all 25 people back to the DJ lab and we crowded in to learn our fates. They decided to share scores in the order of the performances. I heard my feedback first.

My heart beat quite fast as I looked down but listened closely. Overall, they said I had a very strong set and just needed to work on my microphone skills. I realized I had passed the class with a very high score. My classmates gave me much love and congratulations. The instructors proceeded to go down the rest of the list of the students.

There were some surprises and people who thought they had passed but did not. There was shouting, tears of anger, and tears of joy as the announcements continued on. I remember my good friend DJ Flossy texting Just Hector and me to see what our scores were. Even my friend Eli M was nervous for me because she had witnessed my pain from not passing before.

Finally, the reveal was done, and we could leave. There was no alumni reception after this exam but I didn't care. I was so happy and proud of myself. I had stuck with it and crushed that class. I ended up getting one of the highest total scores ever.

The second time through was a definite growing experience personally and professionally, and my confidence in my abilities as a DJ were off the charts. If I ever meet you at an event, please remind me to share with you the speech that the director of the program (DJ Hapa) made about me at graduation. I keep it on my phone and still watch it on days when I am down or suffering through a rough patch.

I wish I could have called my dad and shared the good news with him. He was watching from above, though. That gives me a small bit of solace.

Conclusion

I promised to take you through a night as a DJ at a popular club in Hollywood, California through the eyes of a DJ. We experienced a night full of highs, lows, and learning experiences along the way. You were exposed to songs you recognized and a few songs that you may have forgotten about.

Now you can recognize the parallel between the time periods of a DJ set and the stages a business goes through. Perhaps now you will understand why a DJ can't (or won't) play all of the hits as soon as you arrive at the club. There is a method to the madness. You also now know that there is a lot going on behind the scenes in the DJ booth, even though the music can never, ever stop.

Before the night began, you allowed fear to stop you from pursuing your creative passions and simply taking a risk that you have been contemplating for many years. It is my hope that experiencing the night through my eyes as a DJ (and a business) has inspired you to take a risk, put fear in the corner, and open yourself up to the possibilities in front of you. As I did, you may experience some short-term disappointment and maybe even trip and fall (Hello,

Scratch Academy!), but the long-term benefits will make the journey worthwhile.

I can't wait until you are performing as a DJ (or in business) and get goose bumps the first time you cut the volume and the crowd is still singing along to "Killing Me Softly" by the Fugees.

It is possible.

> *Thanks for being my sidekick, my hype man or woman, and my partner in crime for the night. I hope to hear about your first night as a DJ real soon.*
>
> *—AmRo*

Acknowledgements

I'd like to express my heartfelt gratitude to all of the people who made this book possible. Thank you to Nicole Leone Photography and Heather Leyse for helping me create the best cover photo for my book. To Evolution of Style, thank you for the suit I'm wearing in that photo. You made me look great! Thank you to Book Launchers and all of their team for guiding me through the book-writing process and helping me shape my idea into a polished book I can proudly stand behind.

62071364R00086